SWIMMING FOR LIFE

A Guide to Swimming for Fitness, Health and Enjoyment

Gene Greenberg

PublishAmerica
Baltimore

ISBN: 1-4241-8716-8
PUBLISHED BY PUBLISHAMERICA, LLLP
www.publishamerica.com
Baltimore

Printed in the United States of America

Illustrations by Istvan Diossy
www.cominternetco.com
Peter Caldarone

DEDICATED TO

My children:
Mitchell & Ronda Greenberg
Lori & Jonathan O'Neal
and
My four wonderful grandchildren:
In age order:
Scott Greenberg
Amanda O'Neal
Jessi Greenberg
Robert O'Neal

ACKNOWLEDGMENTS

At the risk of sounding as if I were an "Academy Award" winner I feel compelled to acknowledge and sincerely thank quite a few friends and family members that assisted me in the writing of this book.

I extend a great big thank you to all of the following people:

My wife, Shelly, for invaluable assistance with my unfriendly computer, for typing services and for helping an unorganized person complete this work in a relatively organized manner.

Dr. R. Michael Gallagher for providing the incentive and motivation that encouraged me to begin the process of writing and for his initial guidance concerning the necessary basic skills a potential author must acquire. Michael taught me to relax and be myself while writing which made this undertaking, even more, enjoyable.

Judy Wilson and Herb Block for their initial editing efforts, for instilling much needed confidence and above all for assisting me with the procedures necessary to contact and procure a publishing company.

Dr. Mitchell Greenberg, Dr. S. James Shafer and Dr. Gregory MacKay for their suggestions and assistance with the chapter of the book that deals with nutritional and medical issues.

John Dubon, a good friend that enthusiastically provided his professional and expert photographic skills.

Mr. Gene O'Neil and Mr. Barry Segal, for taking the time out of their busy schedules to provide me with very capable legal assistance.

Marv Greenberg. Always interested in my progress on the book and for constantly supplying food for thought.

Jonathan O'Neal for his ongoing technical assistance and creativity.

Last but not least, as they say, I want to thank all of the swimmers that have taken part in my swim programs, past and present. They have all been a pleasure to work with, are supportive of this endeavor and I consider each one of them a very good friend.

Contents

THE WARM-UP

I want you to share my excitement about an activity that can make a major change in your life. One that has the potential of dramatically altering the status of both your health and your outlook on life. Even though we are all getting older and our bodies are not permitting us to participate in all the activities we pursued in our youth, that does not mean we are condemned to the "couch". There is an exercise that is fun, exhilarating, and aerobically beneficial that will not cause injury to major joints of the body. The guide you now have in your hand provides the answer! If you are reading this book, you must have some interest or desire to use swimming as a means to remain, or become physically fit. I am sure you have read and heard of the many health benefits swimming provides. It is an activity that exercises and therefore strengthens most of the muscles in your body including that very important muscle called the heart. Swimming correctly, so as not to cause injury, on a regular schedule, will improve your aerobic capacity, strengthen muscles, promote fluid motion of your joints and thereby probably lengthen your life and no doubt, improve your quality of life. When approached properly, with some knowledge of the sport, swimming also becomes physically and mentally motivating and best of all, lots of fun. Based on my coaching experience I know there are many people that wish to participate in this sport. These folks do not have a fear of the water and are aware of the very basic principles of swimming. That is to say, they can get themselves from one side of the pool to the other. They are lacking an education in the fundamentals required to swim properly, have no knowledge of what is involved in a beneficial swim program and have nowhere to turn to acquire this information. Many people begin to swim on their own without any instruction concerning proper swim technique or the correct way to structure a worthwhile program. Often, these well-intentioned swimmers plod through lap after lap and find their efforts to be tedious and anything but enjoyable. Unfortunately, this often leads to a premature abandoning of the idea entirely.

These people fall through the cracks, so to speak, since there are very few programs available to accommodate them. We can divide them into two groups. The first are those that wish to pursue this activity because they recognize or have learned that swimming is a great conditioning sport. The second group consists of people that have participated in athletics all of their lives but now due to some accrued injuries or other aging factors find themselves unable to play the sports they used to love. The one sport available to them that can provide the fun, competition and conditioning benefits of those past activities is swimming. Finding a way to get started, however, can be difficult. Little is available in the way of books or videos that directly address these potential novice swimmers.

This entire category of people does not seem to be recognized by the sport and is being somewhat ignored. I am a member of ASCA (American Swimming Coaches Association) and although they are a wonderful and beneficial organization, their focus, unfortunately for some, is certainly not on the novice swimmer. I have benefited greatly from the very important and relevant concepts they have taught me such as the organization of coaching objectives, methods to be used in teaching correct technique, proper communication and how to motivate swimmers so that they will be eager to put in the time and energy needed to improve. In their teaching of how to plan coaches programs, however, they refer to their "normal" swim groups such as age group swimming, high school, junior college and NCAA levels 1, 2 and 3. ASCA sends me manuals, books, and newsletters that are extremely helpful if you are coaching competitive swimmers. I do not see, however, any chapters or articles devoted to the un-coached adult novice fitness swimmer. Rather, this literature is almost always directed at coaching competitive younger swimmers. Occasionally there is some reference to master's swimming but even that is a level up from most of the beginners I am addressing. We do not hear about programs devoted to assisting and training adults that are not necessarily interested in becoming competitive swimmers. These are people simply seeking a proper introduction to swimming for fitness, health and enjoyment. You are the people I am trying to reach and help. I have done this by coaching those I have had the pleasure to meet but for those of you that I will never see I am hoping this book will help you get on the road to swimming for life.

Never in my wildest dreams did I ever think that I would have an urge to write any kind of book much less one that helps people to learn something that will benefit them for the rest of their lives. Many of the swimmers who for one reason or another have had to leave my swim program have suggested, and some insisted, I do this. After some thought on the subject, I realized that a source of information on how to pursue this extremely beneficial activity should be made available to as many people as I can reach. Producing this work then became a goal that I am pursuing with a sense of passion and excitement.

This book is not about me, but knowing a little of my background may be helpful in understanding my motivation. About 20 years ago after a couple of knee surgeries, my doctors were telling me that to avoid pain and not cause any more damage to major joints, namely hips and knees, I had to remove the word "running" from my vocabulary. To stay fit and minimize discomfort I would have to find a non-weight bearing exercise. Starving for some sort of aerobic activity to keep my sanity and perhaps lead me to a longer healthier life I decided to attend a conveniently located Masters swim program I had read about. Being a former competitive high school swimmer, I thought that taking part in this type of program would be a "snap". When I arrived there one evening, there were about 10 or 15 very good swimmers in the pool.

There was a coach, on the deck, giving them instructions in English but using terms that were completely foreign to me. Example: Now go six fifties of drill/swims, four fifties of kick/swims with fins and then four one hundreds on your interval time. This was all quite intimidating and I pretty much decided to shelve the idea. Fortunately, as I was leaving with my tail between my legs, the coach asked if she could be of any help. I explained that I could not swim as well as these people in the group and had no idea of what her instructions meant. I thought I was coming here to stay in shape by swimming laps. She directed me to an outside lane that had no swimmers and told me I could do all the lap swimming I liked, without being bothered. I promptly swam one length of this 50-meter pool and found myself so dizzy and tired I had to get out of the water and go home. At the time, I did not know that this female coach, Judy Bonning, was the United States Masters Swimming "Coach of the Year" the previous year. I kept coming back, staying in that outside lane and gradually began to increase the distance I could swim. I thought I was "working out". This terrific coach allowed me to flounder around for a few weeks and then asked if she could help me with my stroke and teach me some drills that would improve my technique. That was when my life turned around. Before this moment, I never really understood what the word passion meant. This was definitely a life changing experience for me. She started to teach me about proper body position when swimming, proper stroke technique, getting a feel for the water and most importantly, correct breathing fundamentals when in the water. A couple of months later, with her encouragement, I found myself swimming in my first Masters Swim Meet. I was very excited to find that I was quite competitive within my age group and actually won a medal. I continued to participate in the program doing four or five workouts a week and competing in local and national swim meets for the next 20 years or so.

I will never forget coach, Judy Bonning. Even though she now lives and coaches in Australia, I never "cheat" when doing workouts on my own, because I know she is somehow, watching. Another important and fun concept that Judy left me with is that during our training, we never swim "slow" and we never swim "hard". We take the positive approach and swim "easy" or "fast". Because of her teaching, the swimmers I currently coach know better than to use those negative words, slow and hard. Judy and I continue, by the way, to keep in touch with one another from time to time.

After selling my business, retiring and moving to a different part of the state I continued doing the many swim workouts that I had learned over the years, on my own. I was tired of swimming in pool competitions and at that point began participating in one long distance ocean race each year, to keep motivated. Although full retirement was fun for a while, boredom was setting in and I had the urge to do something that would be enjoyable and productive. I answered an ad in the local newspaper advertising for lifeguards for a new swimming facility that the County Recreation Department was going to open. At age 67, I passed the Red Cross lifesaving course and began a new career; I was now a part-time lifeguard.

At first, it was a little intimidating attending the lifeguard course with all my classmates being much younger then my children. The instructor was a great teacher and motivator by the name of Murray Baker. He seemed to enjoy teaching and it was obvious that his goal was to make us all great lifeguards. After passing my test, Murray and the Red Cross recognized me as the unofficial oldest "rookie" lifeguard in the country. While working as a lifeguard at the county pool, I would do my own swim workouts after hours. The pool manager noticed, and asked if I would be interested in creating and coaching an adult fitness swim program. I explained that I had previously swum in a Masters program for many years, had received coaching from three different coaches along the way but had never been a coach myself. I told him I would be more then willing to give it a try. Now another new career was beginning. This was perfect; I could continue with my passion for swimming and be productive in doing so. That was the start of a program that very quickly grew from merely one participant to over 50 swimmers. Before entering into this endeavor, ninety per cent of this group had never before heard the words swim workout and certainly had no idea of what constituted a worthwhile swim program. All of them knew how to swim but were in need of help with stroke and breathing techniques and some sort of structured routines to follow. This is typical of the category of people I mentioned earlier that desire to do some meaningful swim training but is virtually being ignored by the sport.

There is a very limited number of swimming programs or instructional books that cater to those who know how to swim but want more out of the activity then just swimming one boring lap after another. These are people that have never had help with their swim technique and certainly have never been exposed to swim workouts that improve your swimming, as well as, provide the necessary tools to make sure you will reap the many benefits this sport is capable of providing. These folks simply lack some coaching on swim technique and a source for a good variety of interesting and beneficial workouts to do.

After coaching this great group of people for a couple of years at the North County pool I decided to move to a private club in Vero Beach, the city I live in. They had recently built a new lap pool and wanted to initiate an adult fitness swim program. Although I felt bad about leaving the swimmers I had been working with, they were all doing quite well and it would be fun to introduce new eager swimmers to instructional swim workouts.

At the new pool, I began working with people ranging in age from approximately 30 to 73 years old. The group was a mix of novice swimmers, new and experienced triathletes looking to improve their efficiency in the water and people that previously swam competitively and were looking to get back into good physical condition.

Once the fundamentals are mastered, it is absolutely amazing to see how quickly everyone progresses and how much the new swimmers enjoy the sport. I know that there are those of you reading now who, with a little help, can discover a great new fun way to get in the best shape of your life. I sincerely hope this book is going to help you get started. I am thoroughly enjoying what I do and continue to receive tremendous satisfaction in helping people find a path to a fantastic exercise that they will enjoy for the rest of their lives. An example I would like to tell you about is a 73-year-old gentleman by the name of Eric Ott who is the oldest person I have had the pleasure to coach. When he reluctantly came to the pool for his introduction to swimming, he found it impossible to swim just one length of our 25-meter pool. After approximately six months of instruction, and perseverance on his part, his workouts are approaching 2,000 meters. Eric has shed some weight; his aerobic capacity is improving on a daily basis, he is having fun and is deservedly quite proud of his accomplishments. We have also worked with a group of six men and women mostly in their thirties that were participating in a training program to prepare for their first attempt at a triathlon. As is usually the case, they could all bike and run well enough to attempt this first sprint triathlon, but the one-quarter mile open water swim loomed as a daunting challenge. Dawn Lash, an extremely capable personal trainer in charge of this program brought them over to the pool to begin their swim training. Although they could all swim, not one of these athletes had ever received any instruction on how to swim properly. Within three months of learning to swim efficiently and doing workouts to improve their stamina, they all completed that swim without a problem. As they continue to participate in triathlons some of the athletes in this group have improved their technique to the point where the swim is now the strongest leg of their race. With this comprehensive manual, I am hoping to reach and help more people to discover the road to fitness through efficient swimming.

The swim program is now flourishing and after taking some time off to finish writing this book, I will be moving on. At the time of this writing, it appears that I will soon begin coaching at Leisure Square, a City operated swim facility in Vero Beach, Florida. Once again, I will happily initiate a new group of potential fitness swimmers.

I am always concerned about keeping up to date with the latest trends in our sport to make absolutely sure that the techniques I am teaching my swimmers are correct. By constantly reading and researching the subject, I have committed myself to make a thorough study of the sport of swimming. I receive and read printed material from the "American Swimming Coaches Association", subscribe to some current swim related magazines and always seek out swim articles from related sources such as triathlon publications.

While I was coaching at the Indian River County pool here in Florida a few years ago, the Auburn University swim team came down during their winter break to afford themselves the use of a 50-meter outdoor facility without having to contend with freezing weather. I met David Marsh, the head coach, told him about the fitness swim program I was conducting and asked if he would give me some guidance. He kindly allowed me to shadow him during some of his team's workouts. We discussed the newest swim techniques and methods of coaching and he answered all the questions I had. Coach Marsh is a world-renowned swim coach that has authored many innovative books dealing with competitive swim techniques. His Auburn men and women's teams have won a record tying twelve NCAA championships; he was designated as "National Coach of the Year" eight times and has produced twenty-two Olympic swimmers. After 17 years as head coach at Auburn University, Coach Marsh is now leaving to take over the United States Olympic Committee's Swimming Center of Excellence at Mecklenburg Aquatics in Charlotte, N.C. I received a first class swim coaching education from Coach Marsh and best of all; he boosted my confidence level by assuring me that the fundamental techniques I was teaching were correct.

This past summer, I was invited to attend a swim camp at the University of Georgia by head coach Jack Bauerle, another top U.S. coach. Georgia continuously turns out great collegiate swim teams. In the past 29 years, he has produced four national team championships, 6 Southeastern Conference crowns, chosen as the "National Coach of the Year" 5 times and the "Southeastern Conference Coach of the Year" 13 times. Coach Bauerle was recently appointed to coach the United States Women's Olympic team in the 2008 Olympics. Along with about three or four head coaches from some smaller colleges around the country I met and learned from University of Georgia assistant coaches Jerry Champer and Harvey Humphries. Both are very experienced coaches and gave me some great insight as to what to teach, and how to teach it. I was exposed to the minds and thinking of some terrific coaches and learned a great deal about the latest swim techniques. All of the coaches were helpful, accommodating and willing to address any questions I had for them. Again, my coaching confidence was building. In observing these great coaches applying their skills with absolute intensity, I realized the discipline and character they were instilling in these young swimmers. It was a pleasure to watch the camaraderie established with swimmers and their coaches. My trip to the University of Georgia was a truly great and rewarding experience for me.

This book will help you get started. If you are going to continue reading, be prepared to do swim workouts for the rest of your life. I predict that once you have experienced the joy and highs of meaningful workouts you will be hooked forever. It is difficult to explain but you will find that after completing a swim workout that has been mentally and physically challenging, you will have a feeling of euphoria and well being that is beyond belief. Your workout days will be the most stress free and invigorating days of your week. I used to be a runner and I never felt jogging or running was boring. There was always a feeling of satisfaction after a training run but it pales in comparison to the exhilaration and sense of well being I receive when completing a swim workout. Swimming always forces me to remain focused on what I am trying to accomplish and pushes me to challenge my aerobic level of conditioning.

Swim Workouts Will:
1 - Stretch and strengthen all the muscles in your body.
2 - Give you a good cardiovascular workout and therefore greatly improve your aerobic capacity and endurance. The heart becomes more powerful and the cardiovascular system, stronger and more efficient.
3 - Give you the opportunity to develop skills and improve performance.

4 - Afford you the opportunity to practice pushing yourself without fear of failure.

5 - Encourage weight loss if needed, by raising metabolism (the rate at which your body burns calories). You will be shaping your body into how you want it to look.

6 - Help reduce stress, anxiety and tension. When engrossed in a workout the worries of the day will be the furthest thing from your mind.

7 - Build confidence.

8 - Allow you to exercise vigorously even as you grow older.

9 - Probably allow you to live a longer and healthier life.

10 - Eliminate the boredom of lap swimming.

Recently in a swim magazine, there was an article about Mr. Jim Press, the president and chief operating officer of Toyota Motors Sales, USA, Inc. Here is his feeling about this sport, and I quote,"To me, swimming is not just a sport, but a way of life. It centers you, builds discipline, gives you a sense of accomplishment, boosts your self image and it makes you more effective with your time. The health benefits are the icing on the cake."

The best aspect of all this is that you will improve your health and life without punishing the major weight bearing joints such as knees and hips or stressing the lumbar spine. You will not be pounding on them while performing this activity. You will not have to deal with blisters or shin splints that jogging and running often produce. At this point, I should mention however, that as a swimmer, you are requesting your shoulders to work more than they ever have in the past. When swimming a thousand yards, each shoulder will turn over anywhere from 800 to 1,200 hundred times. To protect and avoid injuries to your shoulders it is imperative that you swim with proper technique. Strengthening the shoulder muscle groups with some dry land exercises using light weights and/or stretch cords is also helpful.

The problem with simply going to the pool and swimming some laps, although somewhat helpful (better then doing nothing), is that you are not maximizing all the amazing benefits you can derive from this activity. Many people with good intentions have started to swim laps and quit after a relatively short period of time. The usual reason given for this is "wow, is that boring," and it really is. It is so tedious that after swimming a given amount, many good swimmers start to think they have to stop because they are getting tired when the real reason for stopping is boredom. Lap swimming, without some instruction on correct technique will also hinder improvement because you will be repeating poor swim habits and training your muscles to continue to swim inefficiently. "Muscles have great memories" and these bad habits will get tougher and tougher to break in the future. Practice makes habit, not necessarily, perfection. Developing skills is a result of practicing perfection. Practicing skills incorrectly will obviously lead to the creation of very bad habits. Swimming poorly will make you more fatigued and leave the door open to the possibility of an injury occurring. All of this can be very discouraging and self-defeating. Swimming with proper technique will allow you to derive the greatest benefits the sport can provide and greatly reduce the risk of any type of injury. The efficiency gained by swimming with good technique enables you to improve and attain the results you deserve, for putting in the time and effort. This is our goal.

One of the keys to a successful swim program is the varying of your workouts. We are going to provide workouts for you that will not only eliminate the boredom factor but will surely introduce a challenge factor. To insure a continuous improvement of your fitness level you cannot remain in your comfort zone. The people I coach are tired of hearing me say, "You have to get out of your comfort zone" to achieve the greatest benefit. Swimming distances that are comfortable, at speeds that are easy for you to attain and hold, will certainly help to increase your aerobic capacity, strengthen muscles, control body weight etc., but only up to a point. The problem is that the gains you are achieving will not continue to increase. Our bodies are amazingly efficient and in a short period will adapt to that type of relaxed workout. When we arrive at this point, we have to "get out of our comfort zone" and begin to step up to the next level. Just as a muscle grows larger when you stress it by lifting weights, pushing yourself during swim workouts will result in an increase of strength and your body's ability to absorb and convert oxygen into energy. When adding some stress on the system your body also begins to learn to tolerate such things as oxygen deprivation and the introduction of lactic acid that your hard working muscles will produce. The effect of the introduction of lactic acid is to create a burning sensation when working a muscle beyond the limits to which it is accustomed. This is all part of the conditioning process. As mentioned in the list of benefits, during workouts you can try to push to the next level without fear of failure.

We all learn to approach our workouts with the positive attitude of what it is that I can accomplish today. The only failure is failing to try. I am quite sure that this is true in all sports as well as other endeavors be they physical or mental.

The big question is how does the average person go about learning proper swim technique and find good fitness workouts to use?

You can go to the library or bookstores to try to acquire some of this information and/or guidance and you will find plenty of instructional books for non-swimmers and many books written by swim coaches geared to helping highly competitive swimmers and their coaches. There is virtually little or nothing available that teaches the novice fitness swimmer to understand a worthwhile swim workout program and that provides such a program.

Another approach to getting involved in doing swim workouts is to locate a "Masters" swim program, if there is one, in your area. United States Masters Swimming (USMS), www.usms.org, is a national organization that provides organized workouts, competition and clinics for adults over the age of 18. The organization is broken down into some 500-area clubs and currently has over 40,000 members. USMS provides opportunities to attend structured workouts and to compete in pool and open water races against people in your own age group at the local, state, national and international levels. You might find a Masters club in your neighborhood with a coach that is willing to work with a novice whose goal is to improve fitness, and that would be perfect. At the beginning of this quest, however, you will probably find most of these clubs to be a bit intimidating. I hope that by reading and following the advice given on these pages you will be able to acquire a satisfying introduction to this sport. As you begin to build some confidence, I definitely recommend that you, at least look into, joining up with a local Masters Club, if available in your area. There are many advantages to working out with other people and most of these programs do have coaches to assist you. They do not require you to swim competitively but it is something you could aspire to. After following our manual for even, a short period, visiting a local Masters Club workout session will not create a feeling of intimidation or bewilderment. The language they speak the techniques they teach, the drills they use and the workouts they perform will be quite familiar to you. That being the case, you can base your decision on whether or not to join their program on the important factors such as, what you think about the coach and swimmers, how you feel about the way they conduct their workouts and if their workout schedule is convenient for you.

This manual will give you the basics and place you on the road to physical fitness through swimming. Chapter by chapter we will, go over techniques you should be adapting to your swimming. There will also be a section containing "drills" that will be helpful in perfecting these skills. Realizing that it is sometimes difficult to visualize some of the technique and drill instructions, there are illustrations at the end of each of these chapters to aid in the learning process. For your edification there is an informative chapter concerning medical and nutritional issues you should be familiar with before starting a swim training program. Another section focuses on the equipment you might use and there is a brief but interesting chapter concerning "swim etiquette". The latter part of the book contains a comprehensive chapter supplying all of the information you should be familiar with before encountering a written swim workout. This section will discuss the terms and symbols used when creating and writing swim workouts, which, in turn, will allow you to read and perform these workouts properly. These terms and symbols are, for the most part, universal and in the future, you will be able to follow any workouts you might come across, be they on line, in magazines or other publications. Finally, Chapter 10, introduces you to 16 beginner workouts. The last chapter of the book provides a large variety of varied and interesting workouts to perform. All of them are flexible enough for you to adapt to your own level of competence and conditioning as you improve.

Before beginning the chapters concerning efficient swim technique, I would like to mention the fact that not all coaches adhere to the exact same beliefs on how best to propel a swimmer through the water. There are some basic tenets that all agree on, however, modifying and tweaking of these techniques is an ongoing process. A good coach is always adapting to the level of swimmers he is working with and from individual to individual. In reading many books and articles by very good coaches, I find quite a few discrepancies as to the exact best way to swim efficiently. That is really a positive, not a negative situation. With new ideas and concepts, constantly being presented the sport is continuously changing and evolving. As other coaches do, I take in as much information as I can and then follow what seems most logical to me and more importantly use the ideas that are most suitable for the levels of swimmers I am addressing and the goals we are trying to attain. As noted before, I have gone over the basic techniques I adhere to, with some of the best coaches in the country and they have given me the confidence to move ahead with the teaching of these principles. The swim mechanics taught in the following chapters will make you a more efficient swimmer, permit you to do meaningful workouts and help get you to the next level. If later on you decide to get with a masters program and even begin to compete, your coach might make some slight changes to your technique based on your individual traits and the types of events you wish to swim. At that point, you might also be open to learning correct technique for different strokes such as butterfly, breaststroke and backstroke.

If You Think You Can or Think You Can't, you are always correct!
So Let's Get To It, Now.

CHAPTER ONE

BREATHING TECHNIQUE

The first and most important thing we humans have to learn when trying to be good swimmers is the correct way to breathe while swimming. At their first attempts at swim workouts, joggers and runners usually say that swimming is much more difficult than running. Their complaint is that even when highly fatigued while running you can at least still breathe. A very tired but efficient swimmer can also breathe. When you learn to breathe in the water as well as you do on dry land, it will be much easier and much more enjoyable to master all of the other skills involved in the sport.

As a novice, when I was in my sixth or seventh month of swim training, the coach asked me to swim 400 yards easy, take a minute break and then swim 400 yards fast. I asked her if she was kidding because I would just struggle through both swims, and there would not be any noticeable difference in the speeds of each swim. That is when she realized that my breathing mechanics were not what they should be, and we began to correct that problem.

It is very difficult for a coach to see if a swimmer is breathing properly because very often the swimmer is going through the motions of good technique but in fact might be holding their breath or doing something else incorrectly. As a coach, I often see a new swimmer that I know is in relatively good physical condition, and he/she cannot swim one length of the pool without becoming completely out of breath.

Even if this person appears to be breathing properly, I know that our first priority is to work on proper breathing technique. When breathing correctly you will find that, similar to walking vs. running, if you do not try to swim fast there is almost no limit to how far you can swim. For some reason, most beginners at this sport swim as far as they can without breathing and then take a large breath when they are in dire need. In other words, they are holding their breath until they must come up for some air to survive. I usually ask these people if they would practice that method if asked to walk, jog or run. Of course, you know the answer to that question. Well, why do it in the water?

It is imperative to get into a comfortable breathing pattern. Most people have a more natural side that they like to breathe on, while swimming. Some like to breathe every second (other) stroke, which will allow them to breathe on their comfortable side every time. Others prefer to skip a breath and breathe every fourth stroke, which will still keep them breathing on that natural side. Some swimmers feel more comfortable breathing every third stroke. Breathing every third will necessitate coming up for air on both sides. That pattern is commonly referred to as alternate side breathing. It is my contention that any one of these methods is fine, as long as you get into that pattern and maintain it. You do not want to vary your pattern, i.e.: breathing sometimes after every second stroke, sometimes after every third, sometimes after every seventh and so on. If you do this, you essentially will be back to holding your breath. We are looking for a rhythmic pattern of oxygen in—oxygen out. During swimming as in natural life on land, you should always be inhaling or exhaling. Do not hold your breath! After perfecting this rhythmic pattern, you want to start to be conscious of how much air you are taking in, how much you are blowing out and the method you are using to accomplish this activity. On land, we seem to focus on breathing in, and then breathe out, passively. In the water, it is best to reverse that process. Taking air in should be quite passive and we must focus on exhaling all of that air out so that we are ready to take the next breath. Being ready to accept another breath is one of the keys to learning to breathe in the water efficiently. If you take a large gulp of air and do not focus on getting it all exhaled, you will find yourself trying to inhale air into lungs that are already partially full of air (you are not ready to take the next breath). Continue to do that and you will become breathless in a very short period. I am sure some of you can relate to that uncomfortable bursting feeling. Focusing on exhaling also helps to clear CO_2 that you take in along with oxygen when breathing. An increase of CO_2 in the bloodstream causes a feeling of breathlessness.

An excellent method to practice constant inhaling and exhaling while in the pool is bobbing up and down while standing in shallow water. If the pool is too deep to stand just hold on to the ledge. Bob your head up and down in the water. When your head goes under, steadily and forcefully exhale all of the air you can and when you come up, inhale quickly and easily before going down again. Do these bobs five or six at a time. Practice this over and over again until this rhythmic air in, air out becomes easy and natural. By the way, bobbing is a better way to rest between swim sets then by just standing or holding on to the wall, to catch your breath, because it helps to eliminate some accumulated CO_2. Many good swimmers use bobbing to ready themselves for their next swim.

A word to the wise! During a challenging part of a workout if you start to tire it always helps to focus on breathing out forcefully. Some coaches adhere to the theory that exhaling forcefully will result in swimming faster without any additional effort.

Many people ask me if they should be blowing air out through their nose or mouth. That is your option but I will say that as your face is rotating out of the water it is a good idea to be expelling any remaining air, forcefully through your mouth. This serves to make sure all or most of the air has been exhaled and you are ready for that next breath as well as clearing water away from your mouth. Clearing water away from your mouth reduces the chance of any getting in, while you are inhaling.

Another drill to help with the proper breathing technique is to put a pair of swim fins on, grab a kickboard and while holding the board with outstretched arms and your face in the water begin to move down the pool by gently kicking. Focus on getting into a rhythmic breathing pattern by rotating your head, shoulders and hips to one side to breathe. It might help to take a stroke with the arm that is on the breathing side as you do this. Simply let go of the kickboard take a stroke, breathe and then bring your hand back to the board. If this is too confusing right now, just hold on to the board and lift your head for a breath. Lifting your head to breathe while swimming is improper but right now, we have to concentrate on your breathing pattern. Make sure that when you rotate out of the water, you are passively inhaling and when your head goes back down, you are forcefully exhaling.

At this point in your development, the above two exercises will be very useful in training yourself to get into a comfortable pattern of air going in when your mouth is out of the water and blowing all the air out when your head goes back in the water. When this breathing pattern becomes natural and not something you have to battle with, you are ready to start incorporating this technique with the other skills involved in a proper swim stroke.

Good breathing technique dictates that you roll or rotate your head, shoulders and hips as a unit when rolling up to breathe. Do not turn your head, alone, when rolling up to breathe and you certainly do not want to lift your head for a breath. While rotating to breathe keep your head down and do not allow the side of your face to lose contact with the water. One method to help accomplish this is to have the side of your head make some contact with the arm that is extending forward as you are going in to your rotation. Example: If you were going to start your rotation to breathe on your right side, the left arm would be moving forward and extending out ahead of you. The left side of your head should make some contact with that left shoulder. If you are encountering a problem with keeping the head down try tucking your chin a little closer to your chest.

Illustrations 01A & 01B at the end of this chapter demonstrate a side and head-on view of a good breathing position.

AVOID THE FOUR MOST COMMON ERRORS SWIMMERS COMMIT WHILE BREATHING:

1. **LIFTING** THE HEAD TO GET AIR. Doing this wreaks havoc with your body position in the water. A two to three inch lift of the head can cause a five to eight inch drop in the hips that will show up as a ten to fourteen inch drop of the feet. Swimming with your feet fourteen inches below the front of your body is like swimming up hill, a very difficult task and one we definitely want to avoid. This will be discussed in detail in the upcoming chapter that deals with correct body and head position when swimming.

2. ROTATING **ONLY THE HEAD**, TO BREATHE. We need to be rotating our head, shoulders and hips, as if they were on an axis, together as one unit, to breathe. You can role to the air as if you were going to breathe with your belly button. Obviously, you are not going to actually breathe with this body part but there should be enough of a rotation so that the belly button is facing the side wall. Keep the top of your head on, or as close to the surface of the water as possible, as you are inhaling. Many coaches advise swimmers that only one side of the goggles should be clearing the water when rotating to breathe. If you are rotating to breathe on your right side and the left lens of your goggle stays under the surface it would be virtually impossible for you to lift your head away from the water and that is a good thing.

3. ROTATING **THE HEAD TOO FAR UP**, TO BREATHE. Be conscious of what you are seeing when your head is rolling out for a breath. If at this point, you are looking at the sky, you are going too far. Turning the head that far up will result in twisting your torso, consequently, breaking up your streamline position and throwing off the timing of your stroke sequence. What you should be seeing when

rotating up to breathe is the side of the pool and slightly back. That little trick of allowing only one side of your goggle to clear the water when breathing will eliminate the problem of rotating up too far.

4. **LEANING** ON THE LEAD ARM AND HAND. If for example, you are going to breathe on your right side, you do not want to be leaning on your left arm to help you rotate for a breath. That arm should be moving forward and helping you to roll on to your left side. We want to avoid a lifting motion that will occur if you lean on that arm. When that arm is moving forward as your body rotates to breathe, you will have a more forward motion to your swimming rather than an up and down lifting and bobbing motion. As we will discuss later when talking about body position, when that arm is extending forward you can also be pressing down on your armpit to create better body balance.

Illustrations 01C, 01D, 01E & 01F at the end of this chapter, show swimmers practicing the above **incorrect** breathing procedures. I want you to know what these positions look like so you can avoid them when rolling up for a breath.

I cannot emphasize too much that proper breathing mechanics are the KEY to this sport. Good breathing technique leads to efficient swimming. When you begin to breathe correctly, learning the balance of the skills will come very easily. You might find it a bit tedious to work on this very important first step but when you conquer it, and you will, practicing proper swim technique will be much more pleasant and comfortable. Later, when you are a more accomplished swimmer, and your workouts are requiring you to perform more challenging sets, you will find it imperative to keep control of your breathing.

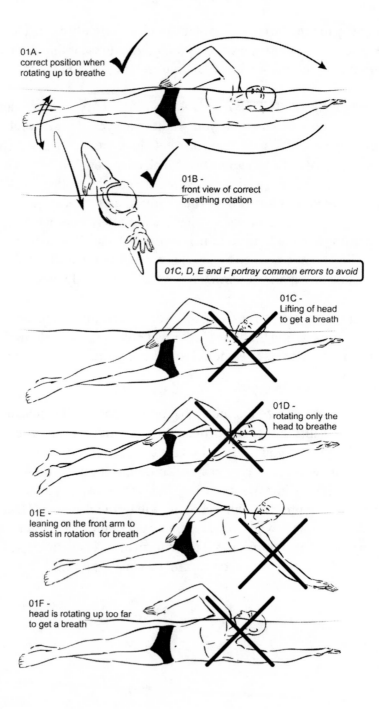

01A -
correct position when
rotating up to breathe

01B -
front view of correct
breathing rotation

01C, D, E and F portray common errors to avoid

01C -
Lifting of head
to get a breath

01D -
rotating only the
head to breathe

01E -
leaning on the front arm to
assist in rotation for breath

01F -
head is rotating up too far
to get a breath

CHAPTER TWO

BODY & HEAD POSITION

The goal is to create the least amount of resistance to the water. We want our bodies to resemble a sleek sailboat effortlessly skimming through the water rather then the flat front, of some garbage barge lumbering and plowing its way along. Be conscious of how your body feels and how the water feels flowing around you. Lying flat in the water, feet level with your head, affords the least amount of resistance to the water you are attempting to pass through. If your feet are riding 12" or more below your head, you are creating a tremendous amount of frontal resistance and it will cause you to feel as if you are swimming uphill. Conversely, keeping your head and chest down will result in the raising of your hips, legs and feet, which will decrease resistance and provide the much better and stronger feeling of swimming downhill. In other words, it is extremely important to concentrate on balancing your body.

Illustration 02A at the end of this chapter shows a swimmer in a good balanced position.

Some basics to remember to attain maximum swimming efficiency:
If your head is elevated, it will greatly increase resistance to the water and cause your hips and legs to drag low in the water.

When swimming with your head down you will decrease the resistance to the water resulting in your hips and legs being elevated.

Minimum resistance = Maximum efficiency

Since the center of gravity of our bodies is near the hips and the center of buoyancy is at approximately chest (lungs) level, the upper body naturally tends to lift and that causes the lower portion of your body to sink in the water.

To help keep our bodies straight and balanced we want to try to change our center of gravity by moving it forward, toward the chest area (our center of buoyancy). The three main strategies to accomplish this are:

1 - Lower your head and chin closer to your chest. Lowering the head, which is heavier then most people realize, will help raise the hips and legs by shifting the center of gravity forward.

2 - Lean into the water with your upper trunk. Slightly press down on your chest and armpit area while swimming. This upper portion of your body behaves as a "buoy" since it houses your lungs, which always contain some air. You have to work to keep this natural buoy from lifting the front end of your body.

3 - As much as possible arms and hands should be in front of the head during the stroke sequence. Accomplishing this will also shift weight forward and therefore help move the center of gravity closer to the center of buoyancy. This point will be discussed again, later, when we talk about being a front quadrant rather than a rear quadrant swimmer.

In the chapter on breathing technique, we covered and illustrated the most common errors that swimmers make while breathing. These errors are worth repeating because these same mistakes are major causes of poor body balance.

1 - Lifting your head, which might weigh anywhere from 12 to 15 pounds, just 2" to 3" while breathing, will cause the hips to drop about 5" to 8" and the legs and feet to drop by 10" to 14".

2 - Rotating the head alone, to breathe. If you do not rotate your head, shoulders and hips together as one unit, it will be difficult to keep the top of your head and side of your face down, and in contact with the water.

3 - Rotating your head too far up to breathe will result in your body twisting out of its balanced streamlined position.

4 - Leaning on the lead hand, as you stroke, will cause a lifting motion rather then a forward motion. The more you bounce up and down the less efficient you will be and the slower you will go.

Your body is going to find its balance in the water. Unless you are one of the few lucky people that are extremely buoyant, you will have to consciously work at keeping your head and the front part of your body down. Without your interference, the front portion of the body will, because of our natural center of buoyancy (chest and lung area) be high in the water and cause your legs and feet to sink. Swimming in this position creates a good deal of resistance to the water and is a difficult task. The tendency of most untrained swimmers is to fight this sinking of the legs by kicking harder. Trying to solve this balance problem by working your legs harder will only result in the wasting of much needed energy. To attain a good balanced position in the water we have to try to keep our heads down and press on our chest. You will know when you are achieving good balance because when doing so, your feet and legs will almost pop to the surface. You will then be swimming without creating undo resistance to the water. A good feeling, to be sure!

During the stroke, the body rotates on an imaginary axis that goes from the top of the head through the spine. Head is facing down with the eyes generally looking towards the bottom of the pool when not inhaling. This rotation is the movement of the entire body from shoulder to shoulder during the stroke. As the hand enters the water, a swimmer rolls on to that shoulder, then flows through the water, going from one shoulder to the other depending on which hand is entering. By

35

rotating as if on a barbeque spit, an efficient swimmer will hold a straight bodyline that does not bend. The most streamlined position you can be in while propelling yourself through the water is on your side. When rolling through the water you are going from streamlined position to streamlined position. The hips, shoulders and head rotate together as one unit as you rotate or "skate" from one side to the other. Your head should not move independently and you want to swim with, what coaches call, a "quiet" head. Many novice swimmers, not only turn, but pull or whip their heads out of the water for a breath. This is incorrect and in addition to being inefficient, may contribute to some neck pain, when increasing your weekly swim yardage. Your head does not have to turn much to enable you to breathe. If the rotation of the head is in line with your body roll, then the head never really turns, it just rotates along with your body. Here again, you can visualize breathing with your belly button. You need that much of a rotation. The 35 to 45 degree role will rotate your body from being on one side and then on to the other side. You should evenly roll to the same degree on both sides. When first trying this it takes some concentration to get yourself to rotate enough to the side you are not going to breathe on (the off side). A correct body roll moves the body from a square-on position into a pointed position, which reduces resistance to our friend, the water. Here we are attempting to copy the way fish swim, which is always on their side. You will admit that fish are much more efficient swimmers than we are so there is no reason not to use them as a roll model.

Aside from an even body roll, keeping you in an efficient attitude and position, it also makes it easier on your shoulders. If you think about it, when you rotate to the side you are going to breathe on, that shoulder easily rolls out of the water and, in turn, makes it very simple for that arm to come out and over in the recovery phase of your stroke. If you do not roll enough to the off side, (the side that you are not going to breathe on) rather than your shoulder easily rolling out of the water you will have to "pull" it out to allow the stroking arm to move forward. The constant pulling of that shoulder out of the water will begin to prematurely fatigue you and possibly cause injury to that joint due to undo and unnecessary stress. We want to make sure that the rotation to the non-breathing side is enough to allow that shoulder to roll out of the water with a minimum or no effort at all. Remember the point of being kind to your shoulders.

Check Illustrations 02B, C, and D at the end of the chapter. This sequence of pictures portrays a well-balanced body rotation. The swimmer's body is evenly rolling from shoulder to shoulder with elbows high and a straight bodyline.

Summary:
When you are swimming, the most important concept to consider is that of being in a streamlined and balanced position at all times. Being balanced and streamlining allows your body to slip through the water more easily while creating the least possible amount of resistance. Think of what your body looks like as it is skimming through the water. Is the water gently flowing around and under you or are you crashing into it? We are striving to make sure your body is comfortably sliding through the water.

You will be working on the mechanics we have discussed in this chapter while doing your drills, during the warm-up period of workouts. Before giving you workouts to perform, you will encounter an entire chapter devoted to the teaching and explanations of these drills. Eventually, the elements of efficient swimming will come together and become very natural. That is when you will no longer be burdened with trying to think about a dozen different technique principles, while swimming.

I would like to mention and give credit to Coach Terry Laughlin, the creator of the "Total Immersion" swim program for bringing many of the principles of correct body balance and position to the forefront. I think that before Coach Laughlin publicized his theories, they came naturally to the elite swimmers but aside from some high-level swim coaches, most were unaware of the importance of these basic principles. It is virtually impossible to teach correct and efficient swimming without incorporating Coach Laughlin's thoughts and concepts on this subject. It would not hinder you in your search for efficient swimming to become familiar with "Total Immersion." www.totalimmersion.net.

Terry Laughlin, the Head Coach and CEO (Chief Executive OPTIMIST) always closes his communications with a great phrase. "Swim well - Be well."

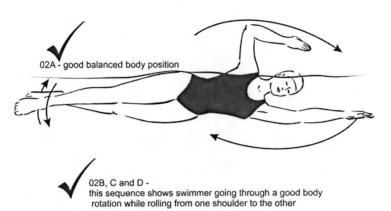

02A - good balanced body position

02B, C and D -
this sequence shows swimmer going through a good body
rotation while rolling from one shoulder to the other

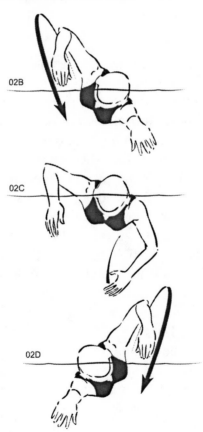

02B

02C

02D

CHAPTER THREE

STROKE MECHANICS FROM ENTRY TO RECOVERY

One of the first things I notice while evaluating or just observing the great majority of untrained swimmers is the very poor way in which their hands and arms enter the water when initiating their stroke. The tendency is to extend the arm all the way out in front before placing the hand in the water. When completely extending the arm before entry, the hand and arm will be flat when contacting the water possibly causing the elbow to be lower than the hand and entering before the hand (a definite no-no). When entering the water with a flat hand the first pressure you are exerting on the water will be downward. Pressing down will not help you to go forward and will only serve to waste energy because you will be fighting against the water. A battle that will only result in making you more tired then you should be. Pushing water down in this manner also leads to the lifting of your head and trunk and gives you that up and down bobbing motion rather then a forward motion to the stroke. This type of flat entry will immediately place your hand and arm in the wrong position for a correct stroke path. Obviously, we want to avoid all of the negatives of a flat entry.

Now let us explain the correct way to affect an efficient, beneficial entry. Hands should enter the water approximately 6" short of full arm extension. The order of entry should be fingertips, hand, wrist and then elbow. A popular coaching phrase is, utilize an "Over-The-Barrel" entry. Visualize a barrel floating directly in front of you as you are swimming and your arm has to go over the barrel before your hand enters the water. When fingertips enter first, and are traveling forward and ever so slightly downward, your elbow will be up (a good thing) and due to your forward momentum, your arm will glide out to full extension just below the surface. This puts you in a perfect position for the "catch" and "pull" phase of your stroke without wasting precious energy. When entering and gliding forward your hand can be straight and traveling in a bit of a downward path. During this forward glide, do not allow your hands to ride up to a position where your palms are up and facing the wall at the opposite end of the pool. This is as if you were driving your car with the breaks on. You will be pushing water out ahead; consequently, pushing or forcing yourself backwards.

Now to the ever present and much debated question of whether the fingers should be held tightly together with hands in a cupped position or with hands relaxed and fingers slightly opened. It seems that the consensus of opinion on this subject is that the hand position should be relaxed with fingers slightly apart. Tests show that a barrier of water forms between the opened fingers and virtually no water is slipping through during the pulling motion of your stroke. Another advantage to this relaxed hand position is that you are not unnecessarily tensing and fatiguing muscles that are not contributing to your forward motion at this stage of your stroke.

Hands should be entering in front of the shoulders. Go straight for the opposite wall of the pool and do not cross your hands and arms, to the right or left when entering the water or when extending out on your glide. Crossing of your hands and arms twists your body resulting in creating resistance and impedes proper body rotation. When your arm and hands cross in front of you, they are not in the ideal position to begin the catch and pull phase of your stroke. Once you commit the error of crossing, an attempt to adjust will tend to create even more resistance. Lastly, a hand entry that crosses the mid line also causes an unnatural and unnecessary twist of the shoulder joint. This is exacerbated by a thumb first entry that further stresses the shoulder area. By the amount of swimmers I see that practice a thumb first entry, I have to think that this type of entry is something that, in the past, had been taught as the proper procedure. Be kind to your shoulders by avoiding crossing your arms on entry and entering your hand with your thumb first. Proper entry is with the fingertips first. If you find that it is difficult to break the thumb first habit you can try exaggerating a fingertips first entry, by attempting to enter with your pinky first.

Illustrations 03A and 03B at the end of this chapter picture both a correct and an incorrect entry into the water.

Picture 03C shows the proper path of your entry arm as it moves forward into the glide phase of the stroke. 03D portrays an arm that is incorrectly crossing in front of the head as it begins to glide out. The main point to consider here is that you want the arm to be going straight for the opposite end of the pool and it should not be crossing to the left or right in front of the head.

Your hand enters, the body rolls downward to the same side and the shoulder pushes forward from the chest permitting the hand to catch water when it is fully extended. These are movements you would use when trying to grab something that is just a little too far out of reach. Be careful not to allow your shoulder to dip too much at this point. You want to be moving forward, not down. As your hand reaches the end of its glide and stops moving forward, you are ready to "catch" water and begin to pull. Catching "your" water should be early or high before your hand begins to drift down too far. The hand position would be such that your fingers are facing the bottom of the pool with a slight bias to the inside. Here the hand is rotating so that the palm is facing your feet. This position will make it easier to pull along side and a little under your body and through to your hip. Do not allow your pull to take you too far under your body and certainly not past the mid-line. As you begin to pull, point your elbow at the sidewall of the pool. This will put it at about a 90" angle. I believe that if you initiate your pull with a high catch, that elbow will automatically be at the correct angle and you will not have to think about the geometry issue. As the arm straightens, squeeze it back to your side. While pulling through make sure your elbow stays high and never drops below your hand. We advocate a straight-through pull, arm stroke. For a long time coaches were teaching, and maybe some still are, an "S" shaped pull. I believe that when that particular technique was initiated and became popular, coaches were not yet focusing on body rotation as an important aspect of the stroke. Trying to perform an "S" shaped pull would probably be a hindrance to proper body rotation. Coaches are now rethinking that paradigm and I believe most are making this change. It seems logical to me that the straight-through arm pull accomplishes the purpose of the pull with the least amount of energy expended and the least amount of resistance created. That is the concept we are constantly seeking. The old KSS (Keep it Simple, Stupid) theory seems to apply.

The arm and hand should pull the water almost directly backward from the chest to the waist or at most, the hip, with the arm bent at the elbow creating a 90-degree angle. When in the process of pulling through, your hand might be slightly under your body but you could favor pulling along side of the body rather than really getting underneath. If you pull under your body and cross the centerline, you will cause your body to twist and lose its streamlined position. This crossing the mid line movement will also create a strange and energy wasting path toward the next phase of your stroke, the recovery. The stroke accelerates as it progresses toward the end. Accelerating all the way through is similar to a follow through when throwing a ball or hitting a ball with a golf club. After a ball leaves your hand or the head of a golf club, it will travel with more speed and accuracy if you have executed a proper follow through.

Illustration 03E is a top view of a high catch and proper path for your arm to take when pulling. 03F shows you an incorrect pull with the arm going so far under the body it is crossing the mid-line.

Summary:
Hands enter the water in front of your shoulders.
Enter your hand about 6" before the arm is fully extended. Forward

momentum will then extend the arm all the way out under the surface of the water and at this time; you are rolling on to that shoulder.

When your arm stops, gliding forward it is time for your hand to catch "your" water and begin to pull.

Your hand should not be too deep in the water when pulling. Approximately 12" to 16" beneath the bodyline is sufficient. Remember to pull alongside and slightly under your body without crossing the mid-line of the body when doing so.

Accelerate the pull as you go toward the hip area where your arm will exit the water, elbow first. You then move your arm forward (recover) keeping your elbow high and remembering to utilize an over the barrel entry.

Efficiency dictates that both of your hands should be in front of your head during every moment of the stroke cycle. Do not start to "pull" until your recovering hand is in front of your head, (the front quadrant). If your pulling arm is past your head before the recovery hand and arm get out front, you are a "rear quadrant" swimmer. Rear quadrant swimmers tend to lose their momentum during the stroke and body balance is negatively affected. To be a front quadrant swimmer you have to make sure you do not shorten the glide on the entering arm. That entering arm is forcefully going into the water and extending out on a nice long glide before it starts pulling back. You begin the catch and pull at the point your gliding arm stops moving forward. Some coaches advocate exaggerating the glide by allowing your hand to stay out front for a bit before starting your pull. In the interest of not losing any momentum, I believe that if your arm is no longer moving forward it should immediately begin pulling back so as not to cause any hesitation in the stroke. That long glide gives your recovering arm a chance to get out in front of your head before the pulling arm has pulled passed your head on its way to finishing the stroke. Right now, you certainly do not have to be concerned about swimming fast. Later in your development, when and if this becomes somewhat of a factor, you will realize that speed is created out in front of you. When you are trying to swim fast is when front quadrant swimming becomes crucial.

See illustration 03G at the end of the chapter, which is a top view of both of the swimmer's arms in the front quadrant. Notice that the right arm which is moving forward is out in front of the head before the pulling arm (left) has passed the head on its path back.

When swimming with a nice long arm glide out front, you are also becoming more efficient in the water due to the fact that you will be decreasing your stroke count. You can determine your stroke count by simply counting your strokes during a 25-yard swim. Your goal is to reduce your stroke count for a given distance without losing any speed.

Let us say, you swim 25 yards in 23 seconds and you take 27 strokes to do so. If, after working on your technique for a while, you can swim the 25 yards in the same 23 seconds with a reduced stroke count of 26 strokes, you have significantly improved your efficiency. If later on you can improve your time by one second but continue to hold your 26-stroke count, you have again improved your efficiency level. If you can lower your swim time, and lower your stroke count - hooray for you. You are doing great! Fewer strokes = less expenditure of energy to accomplish the same job because you are traveling more distance per stroke.

The triathletes in my program are especially interested in this energy conservation aspect. Every two strokes saved in a 25-yard swim will result in a savings of over 120 strokes over the course of one mile. When participating in a triathlon, after completing your swim, you then have to jump on your bike and after that biking leg; you are going to be off on a run. Saving strokes on your swim conserves valuable energy needed on the bike and run portions of the race. Of course, you can, as they say, do the math and figure out your energy savings when you get that stroke count down even further. If you do some calculations you will arrive at the realization that in an iron man distance triathlon where the swim is 2.25 miles, by reducing your stroke count just one stroke per 25 yards you will save approximately 176 strokes in that swim. Obviously, that is a significant conservation of energy.

Most novice swimmers I see are starting out at 30 or more strokes per 25 yards. With the first few major technique improvements that count takes a dramatic drop to approximately 24 or 25 strokes per 25 yards. After that, as you work towards 20 or less strokes, the improvements are a little less dramatic, more on the order of slow but sure. As you are performing workouts, remember to monitor your stroke count from time to time. Reduced stroke count is a good barometer of your efficiency in the water.

Using fewer strokes, believe it or not, also increases your speed because fewer strokes taken to swim the same distance means you are traveling further with each stroke. Untrained swimmers try to increase their speed by increasing their arm turnover rate. Their thinking being that the faster your arms are moving and the more strokes you are taking the faster you will swim. In reality, increasing the turnover rate just causes lots of thrashing around and a loss of proper technique resulting in an increase of resistance and a decrease of speed. The correct way to swim faster is to increase the distance you travel with each stroke. In study after study starting from the 1976 Olympic trials right through to the 1996 Olympic trials it was shown that swimmers go faster when traveling more distance per stroke rather than increasing their stroke rate. After many years of training, elite swimmers can travel approximately 5 yards on a good push off from the wall and then swim the 20 yard balance in 12 to 14 strokes, depending on there size and the length of their arms.

Similar to the game of golf, the player that finishes the course using the least amount of strokes receives the trophy. Invariably, the swimmers that take the least amount of strokes WIN.

Your stroke consists of entry, catch, pull and recovery. We have now covered the first three elements.

On to RECOVERY:

Most, speak of the recovery by discussing the point that you are pulling your hand out of the water when you finish your pull. I prefer to think that the start of your recovery is when you are lifting your elbow out of the water, after completing your pull. The arm is lifted from the water, led by the elbow with the forearm and hand relaxed as they move forward in the recovery stage and is once again, headed to the entry.

On the illustration pages, 03H displays a swimmer properly initiating the recovery phase of the stroke. Elbow is high and as the arm and hand come out of the water, they are in a relaxed attitude while commencing with their movement forward.

The elbow is always above the hand and arm through this phase. A couple of reasons for coaches always preaching about high elbows are:

1 - The high elbow position helps keep body part movements inside the flow line. You want to be swimming in your "tube", so to speak. In our world, the tube refers to the narrow opening in the water through which an efficient swimmer travels. All movements are compacted and keeping you in a streamlined position as you flow through the water. Swimming in your "tube" is also a balance issue. If one of your arm swings out wide, a leg swinging out in the opposite direction will no doubt counter it. This will of course cause your legs to separate while kicking. Keeping your elbow above your hand minimizes arm and leg swing, which helps to keep you streamlined in your tube.

2 - The mechanics of lifting the arm and hand with the elbow uses a completely different set of muscles then those used to power your hand and arm while pulling through the water. Keeping that elbow high allows those powering muscles to relax and recover. A drill you will be performing called the "puppet" drill will help to teach and emphasize the relaxation of these power muscles during this phase of the stroke.

In summarizing let us think about the "TIMING" involved in the sequence of events taking place through the stroke phase. The arms, legs and breathing are coordinated with the body roll. The entry arm extends forward as the other arm is completing the pull phase of the stroke. This allows your body to rotate on to your side where it achieves the most streamlined position. Maintain an even kick with ankles close together throughout the stroke cycle. When your hand and arm "catch" and begin to pull through, on the side you are going to breathe on, you begin the body rotation that will put you in the proper position for a breath. The actual breathing occurs as the lead arm and hand are about to enter the water and the opposite arm is pulling passed your face progressing toward the finish of your stroke. Your head remains flat in the water with the lower ear and one side of your goggle submerged.

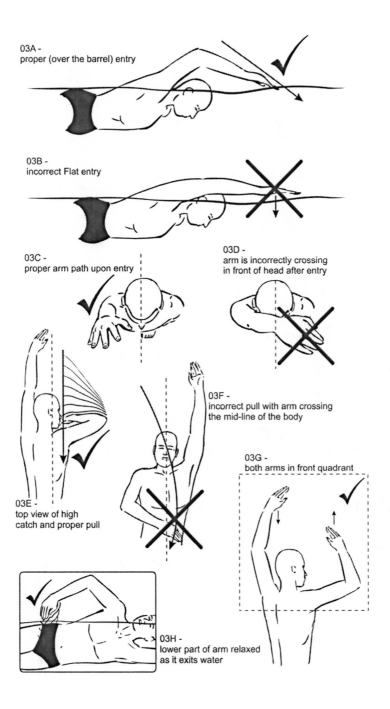

03A -
proper (over the barrel) entry

03B -
incorrect Flat entry

03C -
proper arm path upon entry

03D -
arm is incorrectly crossing
in front of head after entry

03F -
incorrect pull with arm crossing
the mid-line of the body

03G -
both arms in front quadrant

03E -
top view of high
catch and proper pull

03H -
lower part of arm relaxed
as it exits water

CHAPTER FOUR

KICKING

In our fitness workouts, we are concentrating on the freestyle stroke, sometimes referred to as the crawl. Therefore, we are focusing on the kick you would use when executing this stroke, namely, the freestyle or flutter kick. Later in this chapter, we will briefly touch on some other kicks you can use when kicking is called for during the warm-up period of any given workout.

The basic motion of the flutter kick used in freestyle swimming is alternately separating the legs and feet and then drawing them back together. The drawing of the legs and feet back together is what produces the force, which helps propel the swimmer forward. When kicking fast you want to be percolating or churning the water, so do not allow your legs to separate too far and go too deep or too high out of the water. By separating them too much you are making it more difficult for them to come together again and create the desired power. The large muscle groups around your hips and butt are the muscles that create the true power in your kick. The common error, of a large knee bend when kicking, is counteracting the work of these power muscles. You will be getting minimal results for your efforts when kicking with knees that are bending too much. Allow your kick to start from the hips with the power building and flowing down your legs to very relaxed and flexible ankles. This sequence is similar to walking. Remember not to let either of your legs swing out wide while swimming. We do not want to get outside the tube so keep your ankles close together as they move through the kick motion. Toes should be pointed and there should be only a slight bend in your knees while kicking. To point your toes back you will be flexing your foot past 90 degrees. If you can flex those feet substantially past that 90 degrees very little knee bend will be needed to kick and you will not be requiring your calf muscles to do much, if any, work during this process.

All of that being said, the key, is to adapt the principles of a good kick but to do so with your legs loose and relaxed. Just because you are going to point your toes does not mean that you have to create tension. You can even increase your foot speed while allowing your feet, ankles and legs to be loose and flowing.

At the end of the chapter see illustration 04A picturing good leg position during the freestyle kick and 04B, showing a poorly executed kick.

Two questions always pop up when in a discussion of kicking:

1 - How many kicks should I be taking with each stroke cycle?

2 - Should I be using a two beat, four beat or six beat kick sequence?

For our purposes, it is probably best to not over analyze the subject and focus on having a rhythmic kick that feels natural to you. Trying to concentrate on when to initiate each kick while you are swimming is going to complicate things at this point of your training. When riding a bike or running down a flight of stairs, if you try to analyze and direct each movement, you are bound to fall. This is a syndrome we want to avoid.

For the sake of variety during the workouts and to work some different muscle groups let us talk about some other kicks you can use when your workout is requiring you to do a kick set.

A dolphin or fly, as in butterfly stroke, kick is executed by kicking both feet in tandem, or at the same time. After some practice, you will find yourself getting into a nice rolling rhythm similar to how a dolphin swims. This kick really works your leg muscles and in addition, is an excellent abdominal exercise.

Side kicking is simply kicking while on one side of your body or the other. The body position when performing this kick is to be on your side. The hand and arm of the side you are on, is extending out in front of you with the other hand resting comfortably on the thigh of the side that is facing the sky. You are kicking sideways rather then up and down. As in the freestyle kick, keep everything compact by not allowing your feet to separate too much. Your head should be facing forward and your face is in the water except for when you roll it up for a breath.

Backstroke kick is very similar to the freestyle, flutter kick with the obvious difference being that you are on your back. Once again, you want to initiate the kick from your hips. The feet and ankles are relaxed and flexible and attempt to keep knee bending at a minimum. Both arms should be lying on the surface of the water extended over your head with one hand over the other and for balance sake, lean into the water with your head and shoulders. This position will help keep your legs from sinking.

Illustrations 04C, 04D & 04E at the end of this chapter, picture good position for the fly, side and backstroke kicks.

I am deliberately omitting the breaststroke kick. The reason for this omission is that during our workouts you are generally wearing fins while kicking and I do not think it is too healthy for your knees, to execute a breaststroke kick with fins on. There are many in the world of swimming that think the "frog kick", which is performed during the breaststroke, puts quite a bit of pressure on your knees, and the use of fins will exacerbate the situation.

There are two pieces of equipment that you could utilize when practicing your kick, namely, a kickboard and a pair of swim fins.

An advantage of using a kickboard is that it occupies your arms and allows you to concentrate on working your legs. The board also keeps you close to the surface so that a quick lift of the chin or turn of the head facilitates breathing. If you are taking in enough air, you can overload the legs by kicking very fast without going in to oxygen debt. To take advantage of this tool however, you must use it properly. Most people use the board by holding it out in front of them with their head held high and goggles up on their forehead as they kick their way down the pool. Very often, they are socializing with the person sharing the lane or in the next lane over. Although it is fun to do that and is a nice break during a vigorous workout, it does not accomplish much. When you are in that position with your arms pressing down on the board and your head up, your shoulders will be high and your hips will be riding too low in the water. You will be using your leg muscles to help keep the lower portion of your body from sinking rather than training these muscles to create the desired propulsion.

A better position when using this tool is to hold the board out in front, have your head in the water, and be slightly pressing down with your chest. This position will lift your hips up to a more correct swimming attitude and allow the leg muscles to move you forward instead of just battling to keep them from sinking.

You can practice kicking, of course, without a board. This option allows you to maintain a streamlined bodyline and makes it easier to alternate arm and body positions. An example would be kicking on your side and introducing body rotation while focusing on balance. Eventually, you will be learning to accomplish this by performing a kick and balance drill.

A combination of using a board when focusing on fast kicking and not using a board when you are working on technique and balance could very possibly be the best approach.

I will start the discussion of using swim fins, while working on your kick, by saying that you can use the same approach as with the kickboard. Do some kicking with and some without the fins.

Executing kick sets without fins is somewhat tedious and boring unless you are, by nature, very buoyant. Many people that kick without fins feel they are working hard without much progress and unfortunately, that often leads to abandoning or just ignoring the kicking drills. The fins will make you move faster but if you do not let them do all the work, you will be putting in plenty of effort. Even though the fins are helping you to move faster, they do add some weight, making for some additional resistance for you to overcome. They also make it easier to detect flaws in your kicking, and for that matter, your swimming technique. For instance, if you see or hear the blades of the fins slapping on the surface of the water, you are most probably bending your knees too much. You would then begin to focus on straightening the legs, maintaining a subtle or slight bend of the knees so that you are initiating the kick from the hips. Kicking with fins forces you to point your toes, which is the position they should be in to produce an efficient kick. Another plus is that fin training increases resistance and takes the foot through a greater range of motion. This can improve ankle flexibility creating a more fluid and productive kick. Later, in Chapter 7, which deals with equipment and training devices you will find some suggestions on the type of fins to purchase.

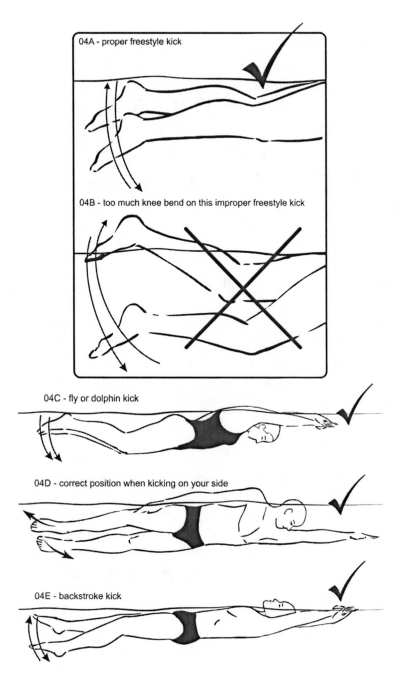

04A - proper freestyle kick

04B - too much knee bend on this improper freestyle kick

04C - fly or dolphin kick

04D - correct position when kicking on your side

04E - backstroke kick

CHAPTER FIVE

DRILLS FOR
TECHNIQUE DEVELOPMENT

We use drills to perfect skills in an isolated manner. In other words, the drills allow you to work on one aspect of your technique at a time. Some are for correct stroke mechanics, some for good body balance and head position, good kicking technique, proper body rotation and so on. There are even drills designed to help you get the "feel" of the water as you swim. When starting to learn the drills take your time and be patient. Although we will immediately be making you aware of the purpose of each drill, on your first few attempts, allow yourself to work on conquering the coordination involved to do the drill properly. Some are more difficult then others but you will eventually get comfortable with the execution and that is when you begin to concentrate fully on the purpose and dynamics of the exercise.

I like to incorporate drills in the Warm-up portion of the workouts. In most cases, when reading a workout it will not be specific about which drill to use and you should be switching them around and performing all of them. Do not avoid doing the ones that are the most difficult for you to execute. You should realize that the drills that are the toughest for you are probably the ones you need the most and you will soon learn to do them correctly. Drills create efficiency, are fun to do and help get you warmed up for the more challenging part of your workout.

You should be employing a rhythmic easy kick when drilling. We usually use fins when performing drills. Many coaches do not advise using fins because they make you go artificially fast and I do agree that some people over-use them to the point where they become a crutch. I believe, however, that the propulsion that fins afford us allow for focusing on the purpose of the drill you are working on without having to be concerned about loss of momentum (sinking). Please use your fins when learning a drill. After conquering the skill, you can certainly elect to do the drill with or without the fins.

I see many swimmers, after learning to easily do these drills, lose their concentration and just go through the motions. You cannot allow that to happen. There is no purpose and you are wasting your time and energy if you do not focus on exactly what you are supposed to be accomplishing when executing any one particular drill.

There are many drills to choose from and I am going to go over those that have produced the best results for the fitness swimmers and triathletes, I coach.

1 - Brush Your Leg Drill. Purpose: To train your arms to finish your stroke close in to your body and not out wide. Remember about swimming in that compact tube without allowing an arm or leg to swing out wide and throw your balance off.

To accomplish this drill simply swim your normal freestyle stroke and as your hand gets toward the end of the stroke let your thumb brush your leg as it goes by.

2 - Catch-up Drill. Purposes: To promote good body rotation and to acquire the feel of a long body position and stroke. This drill, by forcing you to have both arms out in front of you at all times, also introduces the feel of being a front quadrant swimmer.

After pushing off the wall extend both arms out in front. Stroke with one arm while leaving the other extended. Do not let the extended arm begin its stroke until the stroking arm catches up to it. When the stroking arm moves forward and catches up to the extended arm and hand, is when that arm begins its stroke. Continue swimming in this manner. It is not mandatory but I like to get swimmers to breathe on EVERY stroke, which introduces a nice rotation of your body as you swim. Breathing every stroke might be a little difficult for swimmers that are uncomfortable breathing on both sides but this is a good way to begin becoming accustomed to alternate side breathing. As I said, it is not mandatory so if this is in any way diminishing from your ability to learn or perform the drill, just breathe on your natural side.

3 - Almost Catch-up Drill. This is obviously a variation of the Catch-up Drill. Some call it a three quarter catch-up. When doing this you allow your extended arm to begin its stroke when the recovering hand is just about to "catch-up". It would probably be wise to delay doing this drill until after you become proficient at the original Catch-up Drill.

4 - Fingertip Drag Drill. Purposes: To practice having your elbow in a high position during the recovery stage of your stroke. An added benefit is that this drill makes you aware of your hand position during recovery.
Swim your normal freestyle stroke and as your arm begins to recover and move forward allow your fingertips to drag across the surface of the water. Focus on how high a position the elbow takes when your arm is moving forward with fingertips dragging along the surface of the water.

5 - Combination Fingertip Drag and Catch-up Drill.
Execute the above Fingertip Drag Drill in the same fashion, as you would do the Catch-up Drill. Upon recovery, you will be dragging your fingertips along the surface of the water and you will not allow the extended arm to begin to pull until that fingertip dragging recovery hand catches up to it.

6 - Shark Drill. Purpose: Once again, training you to get the feel of that all important high elbow recovery.

The shark drill acquired its name because if you were on the deck of the pool and saw a swimmer coming towards you performing this drill correctly, his/her high elbow would resemble a shark fin cutting through the water.

Basically, you are performing your natural swim stroke. During this exercise, however, as each arm is beginning to recover by moving forward, allow your hand to touch your waste or hip area and hesitate a split second in this position before moving toward your entry. When that hand makes contact with your hip, your elbow will be in a good high position.

7 - One Arm Swimming Drill. Purpose: To focus and physically watch that your arm is performing correctly during the entry, catch and pull, finish and recovery phases of the stroke.

Many of the beginner swimmers are too quick to think that swimming with one arm will be too hard for them. This drill is a lot less difficult to perform than it sounds. Wearing your fins makes it easy and fun to do.

To start swimming with your right arm only, extend your left arm out in front of you and that will become your stationary arm. Move down the lane by stroking with just the right arm. When you get comfortable doing this, begin to watch and concentrate on the movements of that arm. Make sure you are getting an early entry, approximately 6" before full extension. After the hand enters the water, see that you get a nice long glide. When your arm stops gliding forward, with your fingertips facing the bottom of the pool and your hand turned slightly toward the inside so that your palm is facing your feet, begin the catch and pull phase of the stroke. Accelerate as you pull through to the hip area, finish your stroke by lifting your elbow out of the water, and then continue forward in your recovery with your elbow high. You may breathe on every stroke while doing this drill or every second stroke if that is more comfortable for you. Obviously, you reverse things when doing the drill with the other arm. Remaining on one side and swimming with one arm allows you to monitor every element of the stroke. Take advantage of that by making sure you are perfectly executing all aspects of the stroke.

A factor that is at play here is that performing this drill on your more natural breathing side will be much easier for you. Do not let this dissuade you from doing the drill with the other arm. That arm too, needs to accomplish this drill and in addition, it is a subtle way for you to work on becoming accustomed to breathing on your off side. Who knows, someday you might be in an open water swim and "sighting" on that off side might be the only option you have to keep yourself on course.

A fun and constructive thing to do while swimming with one arm is to be conscious of the bubbles created as your hand enters the water and begins to move forward. If those bubbles are traveling up and down, you are probably extending your arm too far before entry and your hand is hitting the water in a flat position. When practicing a correct early entry, the bubbles will trail your hand as it moves forward. You should allow your glide to take you past the bubbles before beginning your catch and pull. This helps to make sure you are not shortening up on your forward glide and there is a theory that says it is more efficient to catch and pull clear water than water that is full of air bubbles.

As a variation of this one arm, swimming drill you could keep the stationary arm at your side rather then extended out in front of you. If you do the drill in this manner, you should then breathe to the side of your stationary arm and not the stroking arm. When performing the drill this way you are getting a more natural body rotation while stroking. Most people find this alternative to be a little more difficult but it does afford you a more natural rotation to your stroke. It will not hurt to try doing the exercise this way from time to time.

8 - Fist Drill. Purpose: Strictly, a "feel" of the water exercise.

Begin swimming with your fists clenched. Take approximately six strokes with clenched fists. Then, as you move down the lane, gradually open your hands so that by the time you finish swimming the 25-yard length, they are unclenched and in their normal relaxed swimming position. If you were going to do this for 50 yards, you would then make a fist again and repeat the drill going back. With clenched fists, you should feel the water on your forearms and will no doubt notice that you are working hard but not making much headway. As you begin to unclench your hands you will begin to feel yourself holding and pulling water as you stroke.

During your normal swimming, you should have an awareness of how the water feels as you are pulling through your stroke. Mindful swimming is what we are about; we are not simply going through the motions. There will no longer be lap after lap of boring and tedious swimming without purpose.

9 - Acceleration Drill. Purpose: To focus on accelerating as you go through the pull phase of your stroke. This exercise also helps to strengthen the muscle group involved when you are stroking.

Most important part of the instructions to execute this drill properly is that Your Arms Never Come Out Of the Water.

Push off the wall with both arms extended out in front. Perform the catch and pull part of your stroke with the arm that is on your more natural breathing side. If you usually breathe on your right side, pull through with your right arm and take your breath just as you normally would at this point in the stroke cycle. When that arm finishes its stroke, allow it to remain in its position around the hip area and now with your head facing the bottom of the pool again, stroke through with your other arm. Now both arms are back and you recover both at the same time, by moving them forward beneath the surface and under your body, as in a breast stroke recovery. Your arms never come out of the water. As each arm pulls through, start easy and accelerate as you go through the stroke. Before starting this drill for the first time, it is a good idea to get accustomed to the coordination involved by practicing each phase of the exercise while standing still in waste deep water. Many swimmers have coordination problems when first attempting this drill. The trick is to stay calm and not to rush as you go through each element of the exercise. Even if you have a little trouble on your first few attempts at this drill, do not give up on it. Once you get it, it is a great drill.

10 - Kick and Balance Drill. Purpose: Practice efficient kicking along with focusing on proper body balance.

Push off the wall with both hands at your sides. Your head is down, facing the bottom of the pool, and you are pressing down on your chest or trunk area so that your body becomes properly balanced. Complete about six freestyle kicks and then rotate on to one side. You now have one shoulder pointing toward the sky and it is therefore, perpendicular to the bottom of the pool. Execute six sidekicks while continuing to press and balance and then rotate on to your back pressing down on your head and shoulders for proper balance. Six backstroke kicks in this position and rotate on to your other side. Take six more sidekicks and then roll back on to your stomach again. Continue this rotation as you move down the lane. You can get some oxygen as you rotate from position to position and obviously, when you are on your back you can breathe freely. All through this drill, you want to be pressing down the front of your body for good balance, which will keep your hips and legs elevated. You do not want to try to keep your legs elevated by using a more powerful kick. Kicking harder will defeat the purpose of the drill and fatigue you.

If you are in a short pool, you will probably want to reduce the amount of kicks in each position while performing this drill. If you happen to be on your back when approaching the end of the pool, please be careful not to bang your head on the edge, a common occurrence, sorry to say.

11 - 7/3/7 Drill. Purpose: Efficient kicking, proper balance and aid in the practice of breath control.

Push off the wall and get into the position of kicking on your side. This would be having one arm extended in front with the other arm extended back, relaxed and resting on your thigh. If, for example, you are on your left side, the left arm is extending out in front of you and the right arm would be back with your hand resting on your right thigh. Head should face forward with your face in the water, eyes looking at the bottom of the pool, and your chin making some contact with the shoulder of the extended arm. Execute seven sidekicks and then take three arm strokes starting with the arm and hand that is back on your thigh. Three strokes will bring you up on your other side for a breath. Now take the seven kicks and three strokes again. Continue taking 7 kicks / 3 strokes / 7 kicks / 3 strokes for whatever distance the drill calls for.

To assure proper balance while kicking on your side during this drill you should be pressing down on your armpit. This will facilitate elevation of your hips and legs and keep them from dragging too low in the water. If you are doing this correctly, you will probably feel some air on the hand that is resting on your thigh because your hips and legs will be riding high in the water in a good position.

12 - Puppet Drill. Purpose: To train the muscles of your recovering arm not to be tight and tense as the arm is moving forward.

Start swimming and as your arm is moving forward in the recovery stage of your stroke, allow your forearm and hand to be very relaxed to the point where they feel as if they were dangling on marionette strings that are originating from your elbow.

Acquaint yourself with ALL of the drills. Practice the mechanics and always be mindful and aware of what you are trying to accomplish when performing any one of these drills. Virtually every workout you will be doing will require you to execute some drills. Generally, you will be the one choosing which drill to perform. It will be to your advantage to learn them all and use them all.

I have tried my best to explain how to perform each of these drills. Illustrations on the last pages of this chapter will assist you in visualizing the correct procedures. We did not picture the "almost catch-up drill" because it is just a variation of the "catch-up drill". The same goes for the "combination fingertip drag and catch-up drill" which is a modification of the "fingertip drag". Please refer to the illustrations when you are attempting to learn and practice the drills.

drill 1:
brush your leg

drill 2:
catch up

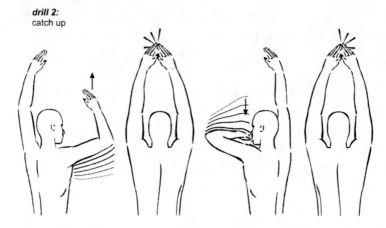

drill 4:
finger tip drag

drill 6:
shark

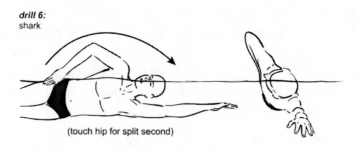

(touch hip for split second)

drill 7:
one arm swimming

drill 8:
fist to open hand

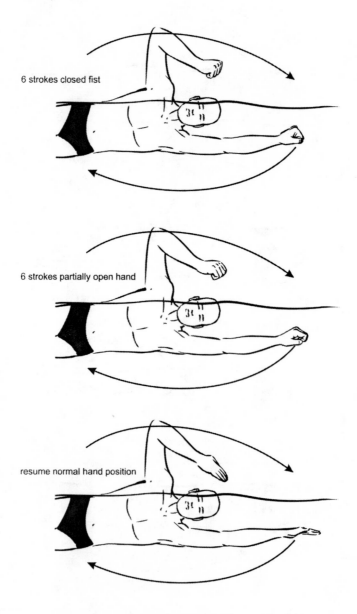

6 strokes closed fist

6 strokes partially open hand

resume normal hand position

drill 9:
acceleration

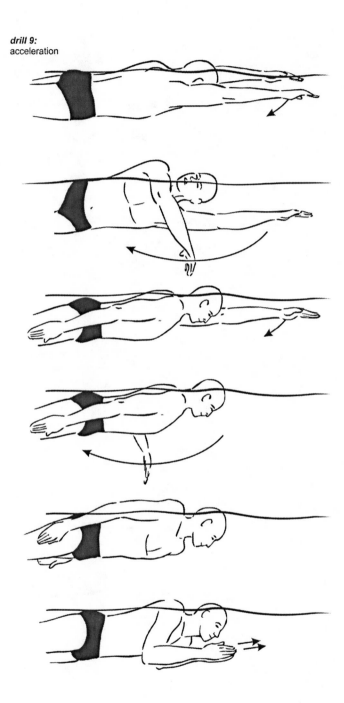

drill 10:
kick and balance

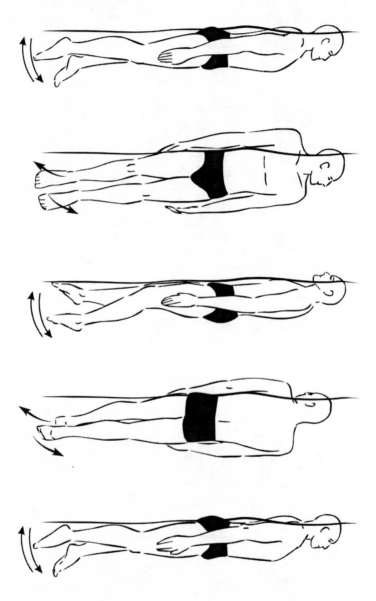

drill 11:
alternating 7 kicks, 3 strokes, 7 kicks

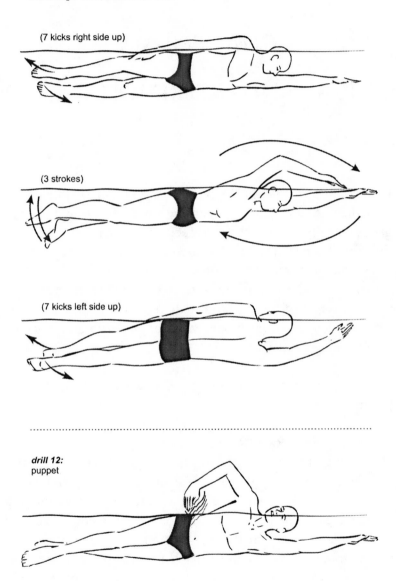

(7 kicks right side up)

(3 strokes)

(7 kicks left side up)

drill 12:
puppet

CHAPTER SIX

MEDICAL AND NUTRITIONAL ISSUES

The absolute best medical advice I can give you is to check with your medical doctor before embarking on a serious swim workout program. Certainly, if you have not been involved in a regular exercise routine for the past four to six months or if you are taking any medications, this is mandatory step.

I am neither a doctor nor a nutritional expert but I did want to have a brief discussion of these issues with you to touch on some of the major, and most often mentioned aspects of health and nutrition in relation to fitness and exercise.

There are three heart rates we are usually interested in when performing exercise:

1 - Resting Heart Rate (RHR)

The average persons RHR is in the range of 60 to 80 beats per minutes with males averaging about 70 and females approximately 75 beats per minute. The RHR is a good measurement of conditioning. A middle-aged poorly conditioned individual's RHR could exceed 100 beats per minute while at the other extreme a highly conditioned, endurance trained Olympic athlete such as a cross-country skier could be at 30 to 40 beats per minute. For an accurate reading on your resting heart rate, it is best to monitor it before getting out of bed when you wake in the morning. As you become more physically fit this rate will usually decrease because your heart muscle is becoming stronger and can pump more blood with less effort and your lungs are becoming more efficient, capturing more oxygen from your blood. During exercise, this translates into more blood and oxygen transferring to the working muscles of your body.

After getting yourself on to a vigorous exercise program, it is a good idea to check your RHR every few months to monitor your conditioning progress. All things being equal, if you are into regular challenging exercising sessions and your RHR begins to go up, you are probably over-training. When starting serious swim workouts, in my late forties, my RHR was in the low seventies and now at age 72 it is 58 or 59. That gives me a sense of great satisfaction and makes all the effort I have put in, worthwhile.

2 - Maximum Heart Rate (MHR)

Maximum heart rate is the highest number of beats per minute you could or should attain when exercising maximally. You can estimate your maximum heart rate fairly well using a popular formula. Subtract your age from 220. Example: If you are 50 years old, subtract 50 from 220 and your MHR is 170.

3 - Target Heart Rate

Your target heart rate during challenging workouts should stay in the range of 50% to 85% of your maximum heart rate. Using age 50 again, as an example, your MHR is 170 and your target heart rate would be in the range of 85 to 144 beats per minute. To monitor this properly you would be measuring your pulse periodically, making sure you are staying in your range. When you are just beginning to do workouts, it is probably a good idea to aim at the lowest end of your target zone (50%) and gradually build up from there. The low end of your target heart rate will put you in the training zone and the maximum point (85% of MHR) is the highest heart rate that is medically safe.

To measure your heart rate, or pulse, you can use a heart rate monitor or do it manually. Water resistant heart rate monitors in the form of a wristwatch are available for swimming. To manually determine your pulse you place your middle and index fingers on an artery that is close to the surface of your skin, the most common being the radial artery found on the inside of the wrist or the carotid artery in your neck off to either side of you Adams apple. After finding a pulse, count the beats for 10 seconds and multiply by 6 or count for 15 seconds and multiply this figure by 4, to arrive at the per minute rate.

When starting on your workout program, for safety sake, you really should do some monitoring of your heart rate. For those that cannot or do not want to wear a monitor or manually measure their pulse while exercising, there is the popular "conversational pace" method. During the workout, after completing a swim or set of swims at a challenging pace take notice of your breathing. If your breathing is highly elevated but normal conversation is still possible, you are in a safe zone and can experiment with pushing yourself a little harder. If you can comfortably sing a song when in this condition, you are probably not working hard enough and definitely want to try challenging yourself a bit more. On the other hand, if you find it difficult to speak when your breathing is highly elevated; it would be wise to slow things down and, over time, gradually work back up to the level of effort you have just extended. If you are dizzy or feel lightheaded after completing a challenging part of your workout or after exiting the pool at the conclusion of a workout, you should be cutting back some on your intensity and if that condition persists, please check with your physician.

When swimming in your target heart rate zone, feeling very tired and hard pressed to go on, is when you are receiving the maximum aerobic benefit of the exercise you are performing. The swimmers I coach, poke fun at me for constantly telling them that when in this challenged position, you want that little voice in the back of your mind saying, **this is where I want to be**. It cannot be emphasized too much that, when you are in this state, you are obtaining the maximum aerobic benefit, of your workout.

As in any other exercise program hydrating, or drinking, enough to replenish lost fluids is essential. During physical training our bodies create an over abundance of heat. To combat this problem we perspire and the evaporation of this sweat helps to rid the body of this unwanted heat. Yes, even though our sport of swimming takes place in cool comfortable water, it does not mean that we will not perspire. The coolness of the water does mitigate this problem to some degree but not enough to ignore the situation.

When swimming in my first open water swim I was surprised and delighted to see that there was an officials boat stationed every mile along the course. When arriving at this boat you may stop swimming and tread water. An official then throws you a plastic bottle containing your preference of water or a sports drink.

The more intense your exercise the more you will sweat to keep your body cool with the negative factor being that losing all that fluid lessens the efficiency of the bodies internal operations and leads to dehydration. The most common symptoms of dehydration are a slowing of your pace, nausea, eventual cramping, chills and worse case scenario, hallucinations. To prevent dehydration we have to take in enough fluids daily to keep our bodies at a proper fluid level on days we do or do not exercise. How much fluid you need is an individual matter dependent upon many factors such as genetic make up, body size and weight, metabolism rate, training schedule, fitness level, dietary habits and environmental conditions.

The current recommendation is that a normal, healthy individual should consume approximately 64oz. of fluid a day. By following that advice, it will allow us to start our workouts with our normal body fluid and electrolyte (mainly sodium and potassium) balance. Even though we are perspiring during exercise, we do not want to allow this level to drop so we must hydrate. If the workout is of moderate intensity and less then 60 minutes in duration, drinking plain water is fine. For longer and/or more intense workouts, it is advisable to use a sports drink that will replace carbohydrates and the two main electrolytes (sodium and potassium) that your body loses when perspiring. The small amounts of electrolytes that sports drinks contain will also boost fluid absorption.

If you are going to use a sports drink choose one that contains no more than 50 to 80 calories per 8oz. serving. Any more calories than that and the carbohydrate concentration could inhibit absorption. It is a good idea to consume 2 to 3 cups of water a couple of hours before working out and a cup or two 10 to 20 minutes before, would be beneficial. During your workout you want to drink 4 to 6oz. every 15 minutes or so. The onset of thirst is an obvious clue that the body is in need of some hydration but you cannot rely totally on the thirst factor to determine when and how much you drink. The thirst sensation shuts down very quickly when you begin to drink and tends to disappear before you have replenished the necessary lost fluids. It is also advisable to be drinking 2 to 3 cups within 1 to 2 hours after exercising. For most people, the general rules we have stated above, should apply. Moderation is always the key word. You do not want to over hydrate and bring about a situation where the sodium level in the blood is too low.

Weighing yourself before and after exercise is a good way to measure fluid loss. After a workout, it is advisable to drink two cups of water for every pound you lose. A popular method to monitor for sufficient fluid intake is to pay attention to your urine color and frequency of urination. Signs that you are properly hydrating are pale yellow color urine that is virtually odorless and frequent urination. This method may, however, be invalidated by the use of certain supplements and/or medications.

If you are on an exercise regime, nutrition is fundamental to fitness. There is a tremendous amount of material available on the internet, magazine articles and books having to do with proper diet. It is unfortunate that some of this information gets very complicated and difficult to follow. The most frustrating and sometimes frightening part is that the material is very often conflicting and sometimes people with a "for profit" agenda, present it.

We do know that a varied, moderate and balanced eating strategy will assist us in achieving and maintaining strength and endurance. As a basic foundation for proper diet we should be eating a variety of foods including vegetables, fruits, whole grain products, lean meats, poultry, fish, beans and low fat dairy products. It is a good idea to go easy on salt, sugar, alcohol, saturated fats and trans fats.

A number of "food pyramids" that can be accessed on line or in print seem to supply the same fundamental information, using slightly different methods. The U.S.D.A. (U.S. Department of Agriculture) pyramid separates foods into five categories, namely, grains, vegetables, fruits, milk, meats and beans. You may access the USDA food pyramid via the internet by logging on to www.MyPyramid.gov.

A word about each of the categories:

1 - Grains

Attempt to switch from the highly processed, carbohydrates in foods such as white bread, white rice and sugar filled cereals to foods with more whole grains as in brown rice, whole-wheat pasta and unsweetened whole grain cereals. You will then be consuming complex carbohydrates, which contain more vitamins, minerals and fiber. Aim for 6-11 servings a day of whole grains in one form or another.

2 - Vegetables

Veggies are naturally low in fat and calories and 3-5 servings a day will provide an amazing amount of vitamins and fiber. Since different color, vegetables supply different vitamins it is a good idea to vary the colors of the vegetables you consume. An example would be yellow and orange vegetables are a rich source of vitamin A. Varying the veggies also serves to make meals more interesting.

3 - Fruits

Once again, varying the fruit you consume is a good idea since they differ in nutrient content. 2-4 servings a day is a good guide to follow. Fruits are low in sodium and high in vitamins and potassium. By eating whole fruit rather than fruit juices, most of the time, you will also be getting the benefits of the dietary fiber they contain. Consuming a proper amount of potassium helps to ward off muscle cramping while swimming or doing any other exercise. Some of the fruits that are high in potassium content are bananas, prunes, cantaloupe, honeydew and orange and prune juices. Sugar sweetened juices or canned fruit in syrup are not terribly good choices.

4 - Milk

Milk and milk products are great sources of calcium and protein. A good diet will include 2-4 servings a day of milk products including cheese and yogurt. Choosing fat free or reduced fat milk products such as fat free (skim) milk and fat free yogurt will reduce your intake of saturated fat and calories contained in dairy products.

5 - Meat and Beans

2-3 servings a day of food in this category is a major source of protein. Included in this group would be fish, poultry, eggs, peas and nuts. Beef contains iron; zinc and manganese, which are highly absorbable, trace minerals. Poultry and fish provide vitamin B6, pork is rich in thiamin and beans (cooked and white) contribute calcium, protein and fiber. When preparing meat, baking, grilling or broiling is healthier then frying.

Try to minimize saturated fat found in animal products by choosing lean cuts of meat and then trim away all visible fat as well as draining off fat while cooking.

Partially hydrogenated fats and trans fats found in fried snack foods should be avoided and try to cut back your consumption of sweets. The healthy, unsaturated fats are in olive oil, avocados, seeds and nuts.

The jury is still out as to whether or not ingesting supplements is beneficial. The supplement industry is unregulated. We do not know how well our bodies are absorbing the nutrient supplements nor do we know for sure, that they really contain the ingredients that are supposed to be in them. Medical personnel and scientists are not sure if these supplements are helping, but many people use them as an insurance policy hoping that they are doing some good. It is your call as to supplement your diet or not but please make sure you are consuming the foods that we know will supply the nutrients and energy our bodies need, especially when following a fitness regime.

CHAPTER SEVEN

EQUIPMENT AND TRAINING DEVICES

We are now going to go over all of the equipment and training devices I can think of that you might use while doing swim workouts.

Number 1, of course, is a suitable swimming pool. I am not being facetious when I say this. It should be a straight pool rather than some recreational shape, preferably set up with lane lines and one in which the water temperature is controlled and, ideally, kept in a 78 to 83 degree range. The workouts you will be using are set up for 25 yard or 25 meter pools. For your information, meters are approximately 10% longer than yards. 25 meters would therefore be about 27.5 yards. If a 20 yard pool is all that is available and you are O.K. with arithmetic you can probably figure out how to adjust the workouts and make it work for you. If you try to use a pool that is less than 20 yards, you will find yourself doing more turning and pushing off the walls than swimming. If you do not know of a suitable pool in your area, access the internet and go to www.swimmersguide.com. It is a website many folks, including myself, use when traveling and wish to locate a pool available for workouts. Enter your city and state or zip code and the guide will supply you with a directory of publicly accessible, full size, year round swimming pools. Listings include name, address and phone number of the facility, along with information about rates and schedules. The site will inform you of, among other things, the length of the pool, and number of lanes available, time of day you may swim and if it is an indoor or outdoor location. Speaking of travel, another great advantage of choosing swimming as your exercise is the ease of packing equipment. The essential gear, a swimsuit and goggles, do not take up much space.

Now that we have taken care of the pool, I think it will be best to break this topic down into the categories of equipment one might **wear** and equipment or training devices that swimmers may **use** while performing a swim workout.

1. Equipment one might wear would be:
1 - Swimsuit
2 - Pair of goggles
3 - Swim cap (optional)
4 - Nose plugs (optional)
5 - Ear plugs (optional)

Equipment or training devices we might utilize during workouts would include:
1 - Workout style, swim fins
2 - Pull buoy
3 - Kickboard
4 - Hand paddles
5 - Pace clock (Most pools that are set-up for workouts have these clocks. If a pace clock is not available at the facility you choose, it would be advisable to wear a water resistant digital wristwatch that has a stopwatch feature. Most sport type watches with this feature are relatively inexpensive and readily available in retail stores and on line).

We will now explain the different styles of each of these pieces of equipment that are available, why you might use any of this gear, where to purchase and, when appropriate, how to make sure you are getting a good fit.

SWIM SUITS. It is best to swim in a competitive type swim suit rather than recreational swim trunks. Swim trunks, especially those with pockets, create a tremendous amount of drag or resistance because they fill up with air and/or water. Competitive suits are more form fitting and more conducive to the type of swimming we do. They come in many different styles and colors and manufacturers use a few different fabrics. Lycra suits give you the greatest speed advantage but do not wear as well as nylon, nylon blend or polyester suits, which are all very acceptable workout suits. If at some later date, you decide to enter some swim competitions you will no doubt acquire at least one lycra suit for swim meets and practice in suits made of one of the other, more durable materials. When looking to purchase a good workout suit in a sporting goods store, swim shop, or on the internet you will discover that, the major manufacturers of competitive suits offer you many different styles from which to choose. If you are not comfortable with a very tight fitting style, you will usually find a category called "masters" suits that are the same as the traditional workout suits but give you a little extra room.

GOGGLES. An important piece of equipment because if you are going to be in the water for an extended period of time the chlorine in most pools and the salt in the ocean will most probably begin to irritate your eyes. Improved visibility is another advantage of wearing goggles while working out. Although there are probably hundreds of styles and price ranges to choose from, purchasing a pair that fits well is not an easy task. The goal is to find a pair that will keep water from leaking in, without having to tighten the straps to the point of giving you a headache or causing pain around the eye sockets. It would be easy if price could be used as a barometer and I could advise you that the more expensive the goggle, the better it will fit. Unfortunately, it does not work that way since we all have facial features that are different in both shape and size. Obviously, we have to find a pair that suits the individual structure of our particular face. The greatest variety of goggles to choose from is on the internet but the biggest problem with buying on line is that you cannot try them on, prior to purchasing. Some retail operations have a sufficient selection from which to choose. The goggles found in stores are very nicely packaged and most people's first reaction is to avoid disturbing this attractive and sometimes complicated package for fear of not being able to repackage, properly, if they decide not to buy them. Get over that and open the package!

Place the goggles over your eyes without putting the straps around your head and look down at the floor. If you can create a good enough suction by pressing on the lenses such that they will remain in place for a few seconds without you holding them, there is a good chance that you have found a pair that won't leak. Now try them on with the straps and make sure they feel comfortable around the eye sockets and the centerpiece that fits over the bridge of the nose feels right. Some goggles come with an adjustable centerpiece and you can experiment with different settings. This feature is an advantage because many times a centerpiece adjustment completely changes the feel and fit of a pair of goggles.

For outdoor, daylight swimming, choose smoked or dark tinted lenses and for indoor workouts clear or lightly tinted would probably be best. If you discover your "perfect" goggles, do yourself a favor and buy at least one extra pair. A good pair of goggles usually lasts a relatively long time but when they begin to wear and you decide to purchase another of the exact style, they have a way of disappearing from the marketplace. I guess this phenomenon has something to do with Murphy's Law.

It is a common annoyance for goggles to fog up during workouts. What is happening, is the little bit of air inside your goggle lenses starts to get warm resulting in condensation. Some brands claim to be anti-fog but it has been my experience that after a relatively short period this wonderful feature stops working. No doubt that this might be caused by not taking care of them properly but most of us, after swimming, throw them in our swim bag and the lenses might be getting rubbed, scratched or taking some other sort of abuse. If your goggles are fogging, there are a couple of potential remedies to try. Forgive me for being crude but spitting in the lenses and then rinsing is the most popular. I always wonder what spectators think is going on, when they see swimmers spitting in their goggles. You can try leaving a small enough amount of water in the lenses (couple of drops) that it would not be bothersome or detract from your visibility while swimming. This small amount of water will have a cooling effect inside the lenses and reduce condensation somewhat. One of my regular swimmers happens to be a professional racecar driver and he informed me that drivers sometimes coat the inside of their windshields with a light glaze of soap to help with the condensation effect. I do see some swimmers employing this practice with goggles. I am just now beginning to experiment with the soap method and it seems to be effective. A bit of advice would be to apply a very small amount and to purchase liquid baby soap or shampoo. Regular soap tends to irritate the eyes. The brands made for babies eliminate an ingredient that cause this or add an ingredient that prevents eye burning. Another option is to buy anti-fog drops. I have had some good and some bad experiences with these drops.

One last tip concerning goggles is to check the websites of the major suppliers of swim equipment if you are interested in prescription or hypoallergenic lenses. They are available and at reasonable prices.

SWIM CAPS are a much easier subject. On the internet or in your local swim shop or a good sporting goods store you will usually have a choice of latex, lycra, or silicone swim caps. I recommend the silicone caps. Putting them on and taking them off is easy and smooth, they wear longer and are simple to take care of. Applying a small amount of talcum powder after use prevents them from getting a sticky feeling and keeps them flexible and easy to put on. I have now observed some caps that go over the ears but I am not sure if they are supposed to serve as a substitute for earplugs. Most people wear swim caps to protect their hair from the effects of chlorine but I will tell you from experience that they are very effective in keeping you warm when swimming in cool weather. Although you might be in a heated pool a good deal of body warmth is escaping through your head and wet hair exposed to the cooler air is adding to the discomfort factor. Under these conditions, wearing a cap is so comfortable that you feel as if you are wearing a blanket while in the water. The lycra caps do not keep your hair dry and are mainly used for warmth.

EARPLUGS. Swimmers that may be prone to swimmers ear or infections or as a protection after ear surgery, use earplugs. There are a few types of earplugs sold by swim equipment suppliers and some are available in drug stores. It seems that the silicone putty plugs that are soft and mold to the contours of your ear opening are the most popular. If you are simply trying to clear water out of your ear after swimming, to prevent swimmers ear, there are over the counter drops available that evaporate moisture in the ear canal. It seems they contain mostly alcohol and some swimmers concoct their own solutions for this purpose.

NOSE PLUGS are another familiar piece of equipment, at swim workouts. Most swimmers that utilize them do so because they seem to have a problem with water going in to their nostrils when swimming. I use a nose plug because of a strange after effect I have after swimming. Following my workouts, for most of the balance of the day, and during the night, my nose runs. I think that this problem stems from many years of swimming in chlorine water, on a regular basis, and I am sure I am not the only one effected by this. For a time I controlled this annoyance by spraying a saline solution into my nostrils after swimming but this no longer provides lasting relief. The use of a nose plug, although sometimes bothersome, is the sure remedy. Once again, you can purchase nose plugs on the internet, in your local swim and sporting goods store or in select pharmacies.

SWIM FINS. It is not commonly known but an interesting note is that swim fins were invented and first used by none other then Benjamin Franklin, one of the founding forefathers of our country. He swam on a regular basis with his fins. Towards the end of chapter, four and five, we touched on some of the advantages and reasons for using swim fins. To reiterate, we use fins when doing kick sets and when doing our drills. For most of us, kick sets are very slow going without fins. Using this device gives you just as good, if not a better, workout and fins make kicking more enjoyable. The case for using fins when performing your drills is that they provide good forward momentum without much effort, allowing you to concentrate on executing the drill properly.

When purchasing swim fins consider the following suggestions. The longer "dive" fins give you the benefits of improving strength and flexibility. The downside is that you go too fast and long fins may change your kick mechanics and rhythm. The very short "Zoomer" fins allow you to maintain your form and cadence but do not give you the advantage of increased propulsion. "Zoomers" are not easy to use when starting out but you might want to eventually graduate to them since they do effectively work the muscle groups used in the flutter kick. For starters, my recommendation is to get a pair of fins that are somewhere in between the length of "Zoomers" and "dive" fins and are not too heavy. These mid-length fins are usually referred to, or labeled as, "workout fins" and there are many brands and styles to choose from in stores and on-line. The largest variety will no doubt be found on the internet but it is probably best to purchase your first pair of fins in a retail store that has a descent selection and one that will allow you to return them if they are not comfortable.

PULL BUOYS are usually made of soft foam or a molded plastic material and as the name suggests, are very buoyant and therefore float. There are a couple of different styles to choose from and which one you select is strictly a matter of comfort. The original style consists of two cylindrical shaped foam pieces held together with adjustable nylon straps and the newer models are one piece of contoured foam. Both styles come in a couple of sizes. Before purchasing a pull buoy, check to see if the pool you are using for your workouts has them available. More and more facilities are keeping pull buoys on hand for public use. If you wish to purchase a buoy, swim shops, dive shops or the internet will be the places to look. You might find this product in sporting goods or department stores but that would be rare.

Chapter 9, entitled "All You Need To Know About Workouts" includes an in depth discussion of why we use pull buoys and how to use them properly.

HAND PADDLES come in a variety of styles. Usually, they are molded plastic and have some short pieces of surgical tubing to hold them in place on your hands. The main differences in the styles of hand paddles are the way they are shaped and whether or not they have holes on the pulling surface. Some are rectangular; some contoured more to the shape of a hand, some have a flat solid surface and others have holes in the surface. Those with holes cut back on some of the resistance you encounter when using paddles. You should do some experimenting before settling on a pair to use for training. Another available device that some claim serves the same purpose as paddles is a webbed swim glove usually made of lycra or neoprene.

Once again, when you read Chapter 9, you will learn why some swimmers use paddles when training and how to use them.

KICK BOARDS. Chapter four, dealing with proper freestyle flutter kick, discusses the option of using a kickboard while practicing your kicking and the proper way to use a board. Please review that part of chapter four. Kickboards are one of the tools that most pools have available for you to use. Check with the facility before purchasing one. You certainly want to experiment with a board to determine if you want to make use of one, when performing kick sets.

A PACE CLOCK is probably not an item you would purchase unless you are swimming in your own lap pool. Most aquatic facilities that are suitable for swim workouts have them out on the deck or mounted on a visible wall for all to use. The clocks come in different sizes, shapes and may be digital or analog in nature. Some are electrical and some, battery operated. The pace clock is a very important and useful piece of equipment. As we will explain soon, the use of this device will facilitate setting and reaching goals. They also provide you a means for timing intervals and other types of swim sets you will be carrying out, accurately. When first beginning to utilize a pace clock I believe it is easier to use an analog style. They usually consist of a brightly colored, sweep second hand and a black minute hand. An explanation on how to read and manage a pace clock will be thoroughly covered, in the next chapter.

You are, no doubt, familiar with some of the equipment we have discussed but on the next page, there are illustrations of some of the lesser-known devices. I believe the above paragraphs in this chapter cover the information you need to know about the equipment involved, when starting on your swim fitness program.

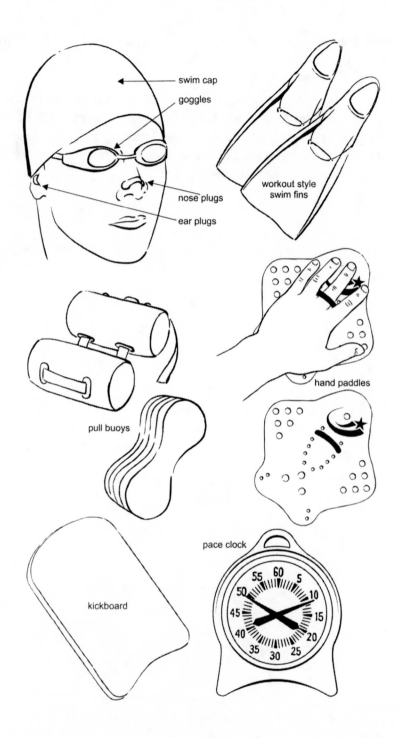

swim cap

goggles

nose plugs

ear plugs

workout style swim fins

pull buoys

hand paddles

kickboard

pace clock

CHAPTER EIGHT

SWIMMING ETIQUETTE

Before jumping into (pun intended) the Chapter of the book that is going to prepare you to begin your training, I want you to know that there is such a thing as pool etiquette. Swimming at pools where people are doing workouts requires you to have a sense of awareness of what is going on around you. After that, you need to apply some common sense, politeness and communication skills. I have never come across a group of workout swimmers that were not helpful, friendly and accommodating. Through the years, behavior that makes everyone's workout experience pleasurable and stress free has evolved.

Some rules of the road, so to speak, for you to consider:

1 - When entering a lane occupied by others, you should ease into the water, feet first, rather than jump or dive in. Be careful not to interfere with another swimmer. If one is coming towards you, wait until they make their turn and push off the wall before getting in. Avoid entering from the side of the pool and swimming across the lanes to arrive at your chosen lane.

2 - Communicate with the other swimmer or swimmers so that they are aware you are joining them in the lane.

3 - When approaching a pool that is busy or active, look to see if there are any lane designation signs. Very simply, the pool might be set up with some lanes for slow, some lanes for medium and some for fast swimmers. Other words such as, novice, intermediate and advanced might be used instead of slow, medium and fast. When you see any designations, take a minute to observe, and try to enter a lane that in your estimation has swimmers that are close to your ability level.

4 - When standing on the deck before getting into the water make sure you are not obstructing anyone's view of the pace clock.

5 - Swimmers can share a lane by circle swimming or by splitting the lane. With one other swimmer, the two of you may decide to split the lane. A line on the bottom that runs the length of the pool usually marks the midline. To split the lane, you each swim on one side of that line.

If there are three or more swimmers, to avoid collisions, everyone should "circle swim". To circle swim all swimmers stay to their right and swim in a counterclockwise direction. Swim down the lane staying to the right side and after making your turn to head back, once again, keep to your right. It is best for swimmers that are circle swimming to be close to the same ability and executing similar type routines. That being the case, it is easier to keep the spacing between swimmers constant. It is a normal occurrence, however, for one swimmer to pass another while circle swimming. It is best to do this towards the middle of the pool rather then near the ends of the lane where sufficient room to pass might become a problem. To pass a swimmer in front of you, lightly tap or touch their foot to alert them of your intentions to do so. You then pull out to the left, swim by and then tuck back into the right side of the lane. When passing, it is your obligation to note if a swimmer is coming in the other direction and wait for him to swim by, to avoid a collision. If someone touches your foot, be aware that a swimmer is about to pass you, slow down and hug the right side of the lane until he/she has completed the pass and tucked back into the lane. If a swimmer is about to overtake you, as you are approaching the wall at the end of your lane, stop for a second and allow that person to make the turn and push off, before you proceed. When stopping at the end of a lane to rest or get ready for your next set of swims, move to the extreme right corner of the lane allowing the other swimmers to carry on. Try never to stop before you have reached the end of a lane.

It is not complicated. Common courtesy is the key.

CHAPTER NINE

ALL YOU NEED TO KNOW
ABOUT WORKOUTS

During this chapter, we are going to supply you with the information you would need to store into your own personal database so that looking at a written swim workout is a familiar rather than a strange experience. That pertains to workouts you might see in magazines or on the internet as well as the workouts we are providing for you in this book.

You are now going to learn how to change your boring lap swimming routine into exciting, productive and enjoyable workouts. Bob Russell, one of the more recent swimmers to join my program, upon exiting the pool after each workout, **always** exclaims, "Thanks, I enjoyed that". It seems that when swimming laps most people will plan on completing a predetermined distance to swim or a predetermined time they are going to spend in the water. They do not give much thought to the specific purpose of their swim, nor do they have any idea of what it is they are trying to accomplish. This results in a lack of attention. At some point, their mind begins to wander and eventually boredom sets in. If or when they reach their time or distance goal, they usually get out of the water feeling tired and certainly not looking forward to the next lap swimming session. In most cases, these sessions become a dreaded chore because the person does not accomplish enough to warrant the time or effort put forth. In a matter of time, most will abandon this exercise. Conversely, when entering the pool with a structured workout that you are going to perform you are in a very different mindset. The phases of the workouts are compartmentalized and each requires a certain amount of concentration to complete correctly. You are paying attention to one particular set and then you are going on to the next which might be somewhat challenging and then to a nice restful set you earned and so forth. The distance and time have a way of flying by and before you know it, you have completed an extremely satisfying and worthwhile swim workout. One in which you have been able to attain and sustain your target heart rate without subjecting your body to impact stress received during the more popular aerobic exercises.

When new swimmers come to one of my workouts, I usually ask them the total distance they can swim when doing their laps. I then have the swimmers complete some lengths, and we follow this with a brief critique of their stroke. I then begin the process of teaching how to swim more efficiently, using the same principles you have learned in previous chapters of this manual. Next step is to start familiarizing them with drills to help isolate and change aspects of their stroke that are creating resistance to the water and negatively influencing efficiency. Again, these are the same drills discussed in our previous chapter on "drills". Next order of business is an introduction to equipment used during workouts and a demonstration of proper use of this equipment. I then go on to give the swimmers a taste of some of the swim sets they will encounter during the main set of any given workout. That completes their introduction to the program and I usually ask if they are aware of the total distance, they have just completed during this initial session. Whether I am dealing with a swimmer with some experience or a total novice, they are invariably shocked to find out that they have just swam anywhere from twice to five times the amount that usually makes them very tired/bored and causes them to quit swimming for the day. This comes with a sense of exhilaration and accomplishment such that they can hardly wait for their first full workout. They, as you will be, are hooked on an activity that you can participate in for the rest of your life and one that will definitely enhance the quality of that life.

I once had a t-shirt, which I liked so much I wore it until it was in shreds. The shirt had a generic swim logo on it, and read, "You Don't Stop Swimming Because You Get Old, You Get Old Because You Stop Swimming". I love it.

I have been performing these workouts for over 22 years and they are still challenging, exciting and fulfilling to me. I am not a braggart but you should know that people who get to know me and learn about the type of workouts I do, are astounded when they find out that I am 72 years old. My gray hair exposes me somewhat but I tell everyone that the color is to due to chlorine damage, rather than age. This October, I am off to Bermuda to compete in the 4K "Round the Sound" ocean race hosted by Randy Nutt's Aqua Moon Adventures of Coral Springs, Florida. (www.RandyNutt.com).

I will be one of the oldest participants, if not the oldest, and certainly do not expect to win the race but I am going to have a great time and once more experience the excitement of realizing I have kept myself in good enough physical condition to be able to compete in such an event.

If your schedule permits, I would suggest doing three swim workouts a week. You should probably start out with no more then 30-minute workouts and as you improve and lengthen the distance of your workouts the amount of time you spend in the water will increase. Based on my experience, I would say that swimmers improve faster by working out more frequently as opposed to doing fewer workouts that are longer in distance and duration. Make sure you feel that your body has recovered from one workout before you do another. Some of you will need very little, if any, recovery time and some might feel some soreness after your initial workouts. You will improve quicker if you allow your muscles to recover sufficiently before stressing them once more. It is important to schedule your workouts on a regular basis. If you tell yourself, I will workout three times a week, whenever time allows, you will find the only thing that will be consistent, is the skipping of workouts. Based on time you have available, decide on a realistic schedule, whether it be one, two, or three times a week and stick to it. You are in control. It is up to you to swim on a regular basis and to make sure your workouts are stimulating, challenging and fun.

It is now time to define and familiarize you with some terms that will be appearing in the swim workouts you are going to encounter.

Warm-up. All of the workouts start with a warm-up period. A related subject is stretching. Some swimmers stretch their arms, shoulders and legs before entering the water. It is my opinion that if you are going to stretch, you would be better served to do that when your muscles are starting to warm during the beginning portions of the warm-up period. This can be done in the shallow end of the pool or if need be, on the deck. A warm-up is a process by which you are going to prime your body for some difficult work. The goal is to warm and loosen muscles and begin to elevate the heart rate. Your heart rate does not elevate by you mentally demanding it to do so. When you first start to exert yourself and your heart rate is still down just above your resting heart rate the tendency is to lose your breath quickly. A sufficient warm-up period will get you past that point and have you feeling more comfortable.

On a personal note, I became aware of the importance of a warm-up in a startling manner. My first attempt at a distance open water swim was to become part of a 3-man relay team to compete in a race around the island of Key West, Florida. I was to swim the first four-mile leg of the race and after the starting gun went off and I swam about ten strokes I was completely out of breath and close to panicking. With the help of my teammates (my son Mitch and my brother Jerry) in the accompanying boat, I calmed down after about a half mile, started to feel like myself, and began to enjoy the experience and benefit from the training I put in. Later that year I came across an article in a swim magazine describing that phenomenon of quickly losing your breath at the start of a race or workout and of course, the author contributed that to attempting to swim fast without a sufficient initial warm-up.

I have now learned that if you are in a race and for whatever reason you cannot formally warm up, you must treat the first part of that event as a warm-up. If you become breathless, stay relaxed, realize what is going on and calmly swim through it. This is one of the first lessons we teach new triathletes preparing themselves to enter their first competition. The novice swimmers that I coach are amazed to find that they are swimming better and are much less fatigued toward the end of a workout as opposed to the start when they get in the water feeling fresh and seemingly ready to go. In our workouts we accomplish the warm-up procedure with some easy swimming, some swim drills to improve technique, some kicking drills and sometimes, easy pull sets. Performing these types of sets accomplishes both enhancing your technique and preparing your body for some challenging effort just ahead.

It is not mandatory but I highly recommend using your fins for kick and drill sets during the warm-up phase of the workout. As discussed in Chapter 5, concerning drills, the fins will give you enough momentum so that you can fully concentrate on the mechanics of the drills you are performing. When doing kick sets, the fins afford you greater speed and therefore the sets will take you less time, be a lot less tedious and much more enjoyable. In addition, I believe you are getting as much, if not more, benefit as you would if you were kicking without fins. Fins add some weight for strengthening, get you accustomed to pointing your toes while kicking and help with ankle flexibility.

A workout might instruct you to kick a given distance and possibly specify the exact kick you are to do. When there are no instructions as to the exact kick to perform, the default kick is always the freestyle flutter kick. When utilizing a freestyle kick extend your arms and hands out in front of you. Rotate your head to either or both sides to facilitate breathing. If this proves to be too difficult, simply take one stroke when in need of a breath, as you would do when swimming normally. For the sake of variety and using different muscles you should at times, mix up your kicks. You can kick on one side and then on the other. You may kick on your back as in the backstroke or you can do a "fly" kick, sometimes referred to as a dolphin kick. The backstroke kick is very much like the freestyle flutter kick except that you are on your back and therefore most of the same principles apply. When kicking on your back you should, have both arms extended out in front of you with one hand over the other and you should be balancing properly by pressing on your head and shoulder area. The dolphin or fly kick is the same as a freestyle kick with the difference being that you kick with both legs at the same time. Extend your hands and arms out front the way you would when performing a freestyle kick set. To breathe, you may rotate your head to the side, or if you prefer, slightly press down on your hands and with very little effort your head will easily pop straight up for a breath. When you get into the rhythm of this particular kick, you will find it enjoyable and you will be benefiting from a good abdominal exercise.

You may want to review Chapter 4, which discusses and illustrates the correct way to perform these different kicks.

Cool down. You will find that some workouts you might come across refer to this part of the routine as a swim down. Both terms mean the same thing. Your warm-up is always at the beginning of the workout and the cool down is always the last component. You accomplish a cool down by swimming or pulling very easily at the end of your session.

The workout might specifically designate a set as a "cool down" or the last part of your final set of swims might consist of easy swimming or pulling which is serving as your cool down. If the workout tells you the cool down is 200 yards followed by the word, "choice", it simply means you can do that 200 however you choose. You can swim any stroke or pull (explanation of pulling will follow, soon) the distance if you prefer. One of my wise a__ swimmers asked me if one of the choices is to choose not to do anything. The answer is, no. The purpose of a cool down is to loosen up and relax before exiting the water. The human body will recover quicker in a horizontal position then in a standing or vertical position. You will be giving your heart rate a chance to come down and blood will be circulating into muscles to assist them in recovery and help avoid post workout soreness. As mentioned before, in some cases, the "main set" of a workout finishes with something very easy and that will serve as your cool down. During this cool down period, it is enjoyable and beneficial to reflect back on the workout you just completed. Do not neglect feeling proud of yourself for this recent achievement and think about the goals you are reaching or are on the road to attaining. Don't miss out on this time to feel good about yourself, you deserve it.

X. The multiplication sign, "**x**", is the symbol most used in swim workouts. When you see, swim 3x50 that means you are to do three swims of 50 yards each. If it reads, 4x100, obviously you would be doing four swims, each to be a distance of 100 yards. Usually some instruction will follow as to how you would swim or in what form these repeat swims should take. For example, swim 4x50 and within each 50, swim the first 25 yards fast and the second 25 yards easy.

Repeats. If you are completing a number of swims of the same distance, we express that as swimming repeats. For instance, you might swim 6x50, each 50 representing a repeat, with a given amount of rest between each.

Drill/swims, which are generally performed during the warm-up period, are achieved by doing a DRILL going down the first 25 yards of the pool and then SWIMMING back the last 25 yards using your regular freestyle stroke. Usually, if you were completing a number of these drill/swims it would be good to vary the drills you have learned in Chapter 5. When varying the drills do not always use those that are the easiest for you. The more difficult a drill is for you the more work you should probably be doing on that particular drill. Assuming that you are using your fins while executing Drill/Swims you will obviously have them on for the swim part of the drill. If you do not know it now, you will quickly learn that swimming with fins allows you to swim faster. Occasionally, use this opportunity to swim very fast. We are not going to overdo the use of fins while swimming and have them become a crutch but it is a good idea to, once in a while, get the feeling of that speed. You will come to the realization that swimming very fast forces your body to behave somewhat differently and that is something you should experience. You may apply the same concept of swimming fast during the swim phase when performing Kick/Swim, sets and the KLRS sets that follow.

Kick/swims. Same as above except you are to KICK the first 25 yards before SWIMMING back the last 25. Here again, you can mix up your kicks by using some of the other kicks we discussed in chapter 4, such as the dolphin or fly kick, the backstroke kick or kicking on your side.

Kick/drills. KICK going down the pool the first 25 yards and perform one of the DRILLS coming back on the second 25.

KLRS. An acronym for a set we sometimes use during a warm-up.
K stands for Kick.
L stands for the drill you perform by swimming with only your Left arm.
R stands for the drill you perform by swimming with your Right arm only.
S stands for Swim.
Kick, Left, Right and Swim = KLRS. By completing 25yds of each element, you will be doing 1x100 of KLRS. If your workout requires you to do 4x100 KLRS, you would repeat the above, four times.

. **Pulling.** If you were to swim without the use of your legs, you would be virtually PULLING yourself through the water. Since you are not kicking during the act of pulling, the lower half of your body will tend to sink and ride low in the water. Employing the use of a pull buoy will help balance your body by keeping your legs and feet afloat. You place the buoy between your legs a little above your knees, wherever it feels most comfortable. Obviously, to keep it in place you have to squeeze your legs together but it does not take much pressure to accomplish that. The negative affect of squeezing your legs together too hard is that it might cause cramping. When welcoming new swimmers to the group I coach, and showing them the equipment they are going to be dealing with, I always tell them that no matter how awkward it might feel when first attempting to use one, I guarantee that they will eventually get to "love" their pull buoy. If you kick when pulling, you are defeating most of the purposes of this activity and the use of this training device so try to avoid kicking entirely.

The three main reasons we "pull" are:

1 - You will be swimming with just the use of your arms, hands, shoulders, torso and hips and thereby benefiting from a very good upper body workout.

2 - When pulling you are isolating your arms and as in a good drill, you can concentrate on them performing correctly.

3 - The act of pulling helps to establish a good roll or rotation and rythm to your swim motion.

The reason you will get to "love" your pull buoy is that kicking requires a major output of energy. The act of kicking requires you to engage the quadriceps group of muscles, which are the second largest muscle group in the body. This results in a huge expenditure of oxygen. Simply stated, kicking makes you very tired. Most people find they can swim as fast or almost as fast when pulling with a buoy vs. normal swimming and it will prove to be less intense. Although there are times during some workouts when we are required to pull fast we very often pull easy, to help recover from a challenging set that has just been completed. It almost becomes a reward for the swimmers, and that is where they begin to "love" their pull buoys.

The other training device that some swimmers use while pulling is a set of hand paddles, which you learned a little about in Chapter 7, concerning equipment. When employing the use of this training tool, the first thing you will notice is that, you are swimming faster with more power and strength. The surface of the paddle grabs more water creating optimal force in the pull phase of your stroke resulting in you moving forward more rapidly. The very use of these paddles increases your strength by working all of the muscles in your upper body that you use when swimming. Pulling with the assistance of paddles helps to accomplish concentrating on your arms, the extension you get on your glide and, in general, all of the elements of the front part of your stroke. They are an excellent tool to help you become aware of how the water feels as it surges past your arms. A good set of paddles are unforgiving in the sense that they abruptly call your attention to many errors that may be committed during your stroke. When using paddles make sure, your hands are straight with fingers pointing towards the opposite end of the pool. If when entering the water you angle the paddles up, you will immediately feel the creation of heavy resistance. If you angle them too far down the water will catch the tips and you will quickly realize that you are prematurely going into the catch position before getting the desirable long glide and extension. After your glide, easily pressing on the outside of the paddles (the pinky side) they will tilt in and down putting you in position for the catch phase of your stroke. In the recovery stage, if you attempt to move your arm forward without getting your elbow high enough when lifting it out of the water, the front tip of the paddle will catch and cause high resistance. All of those good things being said, I do have to insert some words of caution. As good a tool as it is, the additional resistance they create, cause many people to strain or otherwise aggravate one or both shoulders. If, when using a pair of hand paddles there is any undo pressure created to the shoulder muscle group, you should stop and at the very least, try a different style of paddle. If you cannot find a pair that does not cause some strain or pain, do not use them, period. Paddles are a good training device but they are not worth risking an injury that will cause stress and interrupt your workout program.

Lap and **Length** are words so commonly used by people that swim I could not ignore them. You will rarely, if ever, see the words lap or length used on any written swim workout. During a workout when referring to a particular distance, that distance itself will be used. As we noted earlier, swim workouts are based on 25 yard or 25-meter pools. Therefore swimming one "length" down the pool will be referred to as a 25. Swimming down and back or a "lap" will be called a 50. Most swimmers mentally count in 50s so that if they are going to swim, say a 200, they know that a 200 is equivalent to swimming four 50s. When performing longer swims, this method helps you to keep count. As an attempt at some humor and to keep things in prospective, when one of my swimmers whines a little because the workout calls for a 500 swim, I always tell them not to think of it as a long 500, it is ONLY ten 50s.

While on the subject of distances, when reading your workout the difference between 1x200 and 4x50 is that a 1x200 is a non-stop 200 and 4x50 although the same total distance allows you to stop after each 50.

Set. This is a group of swims, referred to during the workout.

Build. If you are going to "build", you will be swimming a given distance and gradually increasing or building your speed within that distance. Therefore, you will start out swimming very easy and end up going very fast. When told to "build" a given distance it is a good idea to break down the distance in your head and divide it into parts. In building a 200, for example, you can break that down to four 50s and so you would swim each 50 of that 200 just a bit faster. To properly build a 100 you would want to increase your speed in each of the four 25s that make up that 100.

If you are to "build down", you reverse this routine by starting very fast and gradually reducing your speed.

Ladder. This is a set of swims with the distance increasing or decreasing. An example of a ladder is to swim 1x50, 1x75, 1x100, 1x150 and 1x200. You are increasing the distance with each swim. If we were performing this ladder by decreasing the distances, you would start with the 200 and work down to the 50. I am providing this definition of a ladder, for your information and you do not have to be concerned with learning or remembering it. In the workouts, you will encounter in chapters 10 & 11 each set is spelled out and you are not required to remember what a "ladder" is.

Pyramid. An example of a pyramid set would be, 1x25, 1x50, 1x75, 1x100, 1x75, 1x50 and 1x25. In this case, you have increased the distance of your swims as you went up the pyramid and then decreased them as you came down the other side. You may also swim a pyramid by changing the amount of repeats and the distances on each step. 1x25, 2x50, 3x75, 4x100 and then down, 3x75, 2x50, 1x25. Once again, this definition is just for your information. There is no need to memorize it.

Descend. When swimming a descending set you are swimming a given amount of repeats, of the same distance and are required to swim each repeat a few seconds faster then the one before. Descend 3x50 would mean swim three 50s, each one being a little faster then the preceding one. You may take whatever time you need to catch your breath and get ready for your next swim between each 50. I am always reluctant to say that because after telling one of my swimmers he can take whatever rest he needs he jumped out of the pool and told me he will be back the next day. Take a reasonable amount of time, seconds not minutes. Along with being somewhat challenging and helping you to improve your endurance, these descending sets are important because they help you to get an idea of your swim pace. It is important to begin to have an awareness of your swim pace. Obviously, if you are swimming a descending set it is not desirable to complete the first swim too rapidly. When, during a descending set one of the swimmers goes too fast on the first swim you will usually see them glance at the pace clock and utter the famous sound "uh oh". On the other hand, if your second swim produces a large difference in time, say 15 seconds faster than the one before it, you will know that you should have swam the first one a little faster. Eventually, by trial and error you will get the feel of your pace and be able to accomplish these repeats with a three to five second difference between each swim. Some people think that since you are trying to swim faster on each successive swim, this is an "ascending" set. We are referring however; to the fact that you are "descending" the time on that pace clock, you are watching. A favorable example of a time difference in a 3x50 descending set would be, swimming the first 50 in one minute and ten seconds, the second 50 in one minute and five seconds and the third 50 in one minute and three seconds.

Another approach to descending that you might encounter in a given workout is to swim a given number of repeats at the same pace, but the requirement is to "descend" the rest time between each swim. Example: Swim 4x100 and take one-minute rest after the first 100, 55 seconds rest after the second hundred and 50 seconds rest after the third hundred.

Rest Intervals. Swimming a rest interval set is executing a given amount of swims with a specific amount of rest between each repeat swim. Example: 4x50 with 20 seconds rest. In a rest interval set, you are going to attempt to swim each 50 at about 80% to 85% effort. In other words, you are trying to swim relatively fast. At the conclusion of each of the first three 50 yard swims, quickly look up at the pace clock and allow yourself the predetermined amount of rest (in this case 20 seconds), before starting your next repeat. Until you begin to swim fairly efficiently and are becoming familiar and comfortable with taxing yourself a bit by swimming somewhat faster, you should stick to doing "rest intervals" when a workout calls for an "interval" set. Normally, unless the workout specifies "rest" interval, you are going to be performing "swim" intervals. When you feel you might be ready, experiment with a swim interval set as explained in the next paragraph. If you find that to be too difficult, simply go back and continue with "rest" intervals until such time that you feel ready for another attempt at this goal. Remember that one of the great concepts of swimming workouts is that there is no fear of failure. You go for the next level and if you are not ready, take a step back and keep training, with that particular level as your goal. At this point, I do not think you are training for the next Olympics so there is no need to rush your progress. The fun and the benefits are derived in the process of improving.

Intervals. Intervals are sometimes referred to as "swim intervals". The short definition is that "intervals" are a given number of repeat swims, of a specific distance, swam at a determined departure time.

Sounds simple enough, but in reality, intervals are a double challenge. Not only are you beginning to participate in some physically challenging swims but you also have to learn to read the pace clock. For many novice swimmers managing the clock is a more difficult challenge than the faster swimming.

This might seem silly or foolish but it would be best if you would be looking at a pace clock or a picture of a pace clock while reading the instructions on how to swim intervals.

See the illustration showing a pace clock at the end of Chapter 7, which deals with equipment.

If your workout reads 4x50 interval and you have determined your interval to be 1:30, the requirement is to swim four 50s, leaving every one minute and thirty seconds. The long explanation and an example of this gibberish is as follows:

Depart for your first swim when the second hand of the pace clock reaches the 60, commonly known as the "top" since the 60 is at the top position on a pace clock. You then swim a 50, using approximately 80 to 85% effort and look up at the clock. It does not matter how long it took you to swim that 50. Your requirement is to leave for your next 50 in one minute and 30 seconds from your original start time. If, for example you swam that 50 in 55 seconds or in one minute and twelve seconds, whatever the time, you are to begin your next swim when the second hand reaches the 30, which will be one minute and thirty seconds from your departure time on the first swim. You are now leaving for your second swim, on the 30. 1:30 from that 30 will put your next (third) departure time on the 60. You are now leaving on the 60. 1:30 from the 60 will put your next (last) leave time on the 30, again.

To reiterate, when swimming this 4x50 on 1:30 interval set, the first swim will begin when the second hand is on the 60, second swim starts when the clock is on the 30, next swim starts when the second hand reaches the 60 and your last repeat starts when the clock is on the 30, commonly known as the "bottom".

It is important to know your approximate swim times. If you were swimming intervals and you left on the 60 and when you finished your first 50 yard swim, the clock was on the 60 again, unless you knew your approximate swim time, you would not know if the second hand on the clock went around one or two times. If, on the other hand, you knew your approximate swim time for 50 yards was 1:00 and you left on the 60 and after the completion of the swim, the clock was on the 5, you would know it took you 1:05 to complete that 50.

I know better than to quickly brush by the subject of how to use the pace clock, so let us look at a couple of different scenarios.

Let us say that after swimming some experimental trials, I know that I can swim a 50, somewhere in the area of 1:15. I want to swim that 4x50 interval set on 1:35, which will afford me approximately 20 seconds rest between repeat swims. Now that means I am going to leave every one minute and thirty five seconds for each of the swims.

I leave for my first fifty-yard swim on the top when the second hand is on the 60. After my swim, no matter what my swim time, I leave for my second 50 when the clock reaches the 35, which is one minute and thirty-five seconds from when I left on my first swim.

During my 15 or 20 seconds of rest while waiting for the clock to arrive at 35, I can look at the 35 on the clock and determine what the clock will read in 1:35, which will be my next departure time. It would have to go around a full minute to reach the 35 again and then I will add or better yet, count 35 more seconds and see that my next (3rd) departure time is on the 10.

After completing my 2nd swim while resting and waiting for the clock to reach the 10 I will once again count and thereby determine that I will leave on my 4th and final 50 when the pace clock is on the 45.

I am simply looking at the clock and counting by five until I reach that additional 35 seconds. To review the above example, I will leave for my first swim on the 60, the second swim on the 35, the third swim on the 10 and the last swim on the 45. If I do that, I will have departed every 1:35 and successfully completed 4x50 on a 1:35 interval.

A somewhat different type of scenario would be to swim that 4x50 set on a 55-second interval. This, of course, means that I have to leave every 55 seconds. Let us suppose that if I expend an 80% effort I can swim the 50, in 45 seconds. I start on the 60, complete the swim in approximately 45 seconds and when the clock reaches the 55, I go again. For me to leave on my third swim on 55 (in 55 seconds) I will have to leave 5 seconds earlier then when I started the previous swim. Therefore, in this case my first swim is on the 60, my second on the 55, my third on the 50 and the fourth on the 45. In other words, to leave every 55 seconds I have to keep deducting 5 seconds from my departure time to determine my new start time.

Please take a few minutes to re-read and digest the above. I know the explanation is quite wordy and seems confusing but if you take your time and decipher each scenario, it might gain some clarity. Some of you will grasp this concept of swim intervals immediately and most of you will flounder for some time before it clicks in. Eventually, even though you might not think so, you will get it.

An appropriate question at this point would be how do I know what my swim interval time should be? A few trial and error experiments will help you decide what your interval should be for any given distance.

Swim a 50, beginning with the second hand of the pace clock on the 60 at approximately 80% effort. Take notice of the time it took you to complete that swim. Let us suppose that you swam that 50 in 1:10 (one minute and ten seconds). Allow yourself a 20-second rest and set your interval time at 1:30. Remember, that the 1:30 interval time is your departure time, after each swim.

Use the same method to establish an interval time for other distances. An example being, that with an 80% effort you find you can swim a 100 in 1:50. Set a 2:10 interval time, which will be affording you approximately 20 seconds rest after each 100-yard swim.

For experimental purposes, set an interval, for any given distance, and attempt to swim that interval set. If that particular interval is too fast or too slow for you, do a little adjusting, one way or the other. As you progress, interval times will change. Do not be afraid to challenge yourself, from time to time, with a tighter interval. As you become more conditioned, you will be amazed at how little rest time you require between relatively fast swims.

If you are a total beginner, and know, you are currently not aerobically fit and need 30 seconds or more rest between repeat swims, well, that is where you are going to start. We will all have different starting points. I would want you to approach this intelligently, and in a manner that will be enjoyable as well as beneficial. Just stay with the program, set attainable short-term goals conquering one before going on to the next and improvement will be steady and fulfilling.

Health wise, what is too slow or too fast for you? Gauge this by whether or not you are reaching or exceeding your target heart rate. Remember, in the part of Chapter 6, having to do with heart rate issues, we discussed a quick method to determine if you were in a target (safe and yet challenging) zone. If at the completion of any of the interval swims you can speak normally, you are in a safe range. If speaking is a problem, it is time to back off some, and set an easier interval time. Conversely, if it is not any problem at all to sing a couple of song lines in a normal fashion, you probably should turn up the heat a little by decreasing your interval time and/or swimming faster.

When swimming intervals, obviously, you get more rest if you swim faster. Do not let this fool you. Swimming a little easier and therefore getting a little less rest time between repeats, is less challenging then trying to swim faster to grab an extra second or two of rest.

This revelation came to me one year during my annual "birthday" swim. That takes a little explaining. Starting at age 50, the birthday present I always give myself is to swim a 50 for every year of my life on a given interval. I am now into the high numbers and last year I had to complete 71x50 leaving on 1:05 in a twenty-five meter pool. I was able to cruise at a comfortable one minute per 50-swim speed, when getting 5 seconds of rest between repeats. If I tried to swim the 50s in 55 seconds to get ten seconds rest between swims, I would not even come close to succeeding. Incidentally, you are all welcome to join my I.S.B.C. (Interval Swim Birthday Club) and you are the boss so you get to set your own interval time. I am thinking about giving myself a substantial birthday present this year by raising my interval time to 1:10. I am not sure if I am going to be that nice to myself.

If you have not realized by now, eventually you will, so I will expose the fact that it is possible to loaf on your last swim in any given interval set, since you do not have to be concerned with the next start time. Try to resist that temptation because you never know if I might be watching from somewhere. Please attempt to stay on your same swim pace for all your interval swims.

Interval swimming is at the very essence of swim workouts. It is the best method of exercising the heart muscle and gaining a high level of fitness. When performing intervals you are elevating your heart rate to levels higher than those that result from non-stop swimming and this builds cardiovascular fitness. Triathletes and others that swim fairly long distance open water swims know that part of their training is periodically swimming non-stop swims that are longer than the distance of their upcoming race. This is to instill confidence that they can complete the distance and to become accustomed to being in the water for longer periods than their normal workouts. They should be aware, however, that the best way to prepare for moderately long swims is to swim sets of relatively short and relatively fast repeat swims (intervals). The idea is that the short rest periods you get are not enough for your heart rate to drop significantly before putting that heart muscle back to work again and that is the best path to building aerobic capacity. Once you are into the routine and are comfortable swimming intervals, every once in awhile you should challenge yourself to go beyond the limits you have already established. You can always back off and try again later. On a more positive note, when your aerobic fitness improves you can set intervals using less rest time. If you can swim that 50 in 1:00 you can try leaving on 1:05 or 1:10 rather than 1:20. Eventually your body will become tolerant of shorter rest times.

Although you are pushing yourself, somewhat, when doing interval work, you must always remain mindful, making sure to concentrate on both breathing, and swim technique.

Hypoxic. I am not sure it is technically correct to use this word to describe what we do, but in swimming vernacular, a hypoxic set is one in which you vary your breathing pattern. Many years ago, the late, great collegiate swim coach, James "Doc" Counsilman, coined this word to describe breath control sets. Some coaches feel that performing hypoxic sets helps to build aerobic capacity. I am not sure that applies at our level of training. To derive that kind of benefit, it is my opinion that, you would have to swim hypoxic sets that are of a much greater intensity than those we perform in our workouts. I certainly would not be upset if I was wrong on this point and it was determined, that even low intensity level hypoxic sets help improve aerobic capacity. We use them quite often and that would certainly be a welcomed and an additional positive feature. To me, the most beneficial aspect of swimming hypoxic sets is that they teach you to stay calm during a swim and to be in total control of your breathing. These assorted breathing patterns also force you to breathe on both sides (alternate side breathing) some of the time, which is not a bad thing to become familiar with. I do not recommend performing hypoxic sets until you are confident in your normal breathing pattern and technique. We, usually do these hypoxic sets in conjunction with pulling, with a pull buoy. You can choose from any number of different patterns.

Let us suppose you are going to pull 1x100 using a very popular 5, 2, 4, 3-breathing pattern.

During the first 25 yards, you are to breathe every fifth (5) stroke.

In the second 25 yards, breathe every second (2) stroke.

In the third 25 yards, breathe every fourth (4) stroke.

In last 25 yards, breathe every third (3) stroke.

On the odd numbers, breathing every fifth and breathing every third stroke, you will find yourself breathing on alternate sides and on the evens, you are always breathing on the same side. You may vary the patterns but when you do so, it is preferable to use two odd and two even stroke counts so you are not always breathing on the same side. During a hypoxic set it is important to stay in control of your breathing.

Even though you might be breathing every 5th stroke it does not mean that you have to hold your breath for that entire period of time. Stay in control, when your face is in the water; gradually exhale all your air making sure you will be ready for the next breath. When you desire to challenge yourself a bit further, you can try swimming 50 yards or meters of each breathing pattern, rather than 25. This obviously results in you completing a 1x200 hypoxic pull. Although, the workout you are performing will usually be specific and tell you exactly how to perform this exercise, you are of course; free to substitute any breathing pattern you might prefer.

Starts and Turns. When competing, both of these elements are critical. If you should move on to a "Masters" program to become involved in competition, the coach will teach you how to do correct racing starts from starting blocks and correct racing (flip) turns off the walls. When performing workouts, although the start and turns are not critical, you do want to execute them in a manner such that you will create as little resistance to the water as possible. There are many ways to do this and there is no one method that can be considered, absolutely correct. I will tell you how I accomplish starts and turns while attempting to keep resistance at a minimum, during my workouts, and you may experiment and adjust from that point.

You will be starting each swim set from in the pool. Place one hand at the top of the wall with your elbow bent so that your forearm is against the wall. If you are holding on with your right hand, turn your body to the left so that your belly button is facing the side wall and eyes should be looking down the pool towards the opposite end. Now simultaneously, let go of the wall, do a half turn so you are facing forward, drop down so that your head is about one foot below the surface and place both feet on the wall with legs curled up. Push off the wall with your arms out front in a streamlined position. A streamlined position would have your arms out front, pressing tightly against your ears and one hand placed over the other. After getting a good push-off, start your kick before beginning to stroke with your arms. Reason being that when you push off the wall you are moving faster then you can swim and you do not want to break up that momentum by starting to stroke too soon.

There are many ways to execute an "open turn", which is what you are doing, if you are not performing a "flip turn". When approaching the end of the pool reach out and hit the wall with the palm of your hand. Try not to grab and hold the wall. Simultaneously, push back, turn your body so that you are facing the other end of the pool and drop down positioning your head approximately one foot below the surface. Now as in the start, get both feet on the wall, push off in a streamlined position and begin kicking before stroking.

Prior to attempting your first workout, please review the parts of the technique chapters that seemed to be the most important, logical and doable for you. Get in the water and begin to experiment with the presented concepts.

Now review the chapter on drills. Begin to practice and perform some or all of the drills. Remember to be mindful and not just go through the motions. Concentrate on the purpose of each drill as you are executing it.

The workouts in the Chapter designated, as "Beginner Workouts" is a good place to start your swim program. These workouts increase in degree of difficulty, more or less, so you could follow them in the order that they are shown. Those of you that immediately find these too easy, will of course, proceed to the next Chapter.

When you start performing the workouts in Chapter 11, you do not have to follow them in the order presented. I did try to start you off with those that are the least challenging but they are not necessarily set up such that they get progressively more difficult. To change things up and to hold your interest, they are varied as to the type or style of workout. Some concentrate on sprints vs. longer distances and some feature descending sets vs. interval sets and so on. Although each workout presents an A and a B version to accommodate different ability levels, you will be determining the degree of difficulty by adjusting distances, varying your swim times and deciding what your interval settings will be.

The workouts will show all the distances in YARDS. If you happen to be swimming in a pool that is 25 METERS, your workout will total 10% more distance then reported. Example: If you complete a workout that shows a total distance of 2,000 yards and you are swimming in a 25-meter pool, you will have swam approximately 2,200 yards. It is going to take you approximately 10% longer to swim any given distance in meters then it would in yards. If you know, you can swim 50 yards in one minute (60 seconds); your time for 50meters will be about 1:06 (66 seconds). The bottom line is that other then monitoring your swim and interval times, it does not matter if you are swimming yards or meters.

Since we are on the subject of distances, it is my experience that newcomers to this sport are slightly puzzled when it comes time to figure out how many lengths or laps are in a given distance they want to swim. A popular way to make this determination is to break down all the distances into 50s starting with the knowledge that each length of the pool is 25 yards. When we refer to a 50, you know that it is two lengths, or down the pool and back. If I have to swim 1x100, I know that I have to swim two 50s. A 200, in my head becomes four 50s, a 300, is six 50s and so on.

Normally, when instructed to "swim", in any given workout we are asking you to perform, the traditional freestyle (crawl) stroke. The focus of our program is to supply workouts that are varied, fun, and challenging enough to raise your level of fitness. We are not striving to make you a competitive swimmer by pushing the aerobic envelope or asking you to perfect different strokes. However, if you would rather substitute a different stroke such as backstroke, butterfly or breaststroke when performing any of the sets, please feel free to do so. As mentioned earlier, if after becoming comfortable with these workouts you are tempted to try competitive swimming or if you desire to swim with a group, it would be best to attempt to locate a "masters" swim program in your area. In most cases, that type of program will have a coach to help you advance and assist you with learning to perform some or all of the other strokes, properly. If you are eager to take this next step for competition purposes, do not be concerned with your age. In "masters" events you will always be competing with swimmers that are in your age group. Nothing would be more gratifying to me than to somehow find out that some of you have come to enjoy swimming enough to progress to that next level. You could e-mail me and let me know.

Our workouts are always very positive in nature so we never swim **slowly** and we never swim **hard**. Those terms are way to negative for us. During our workouts, your instructions will be to swim **easy**, **moderate, strong or fast**. Easy, moderate and fast are completely self explanatory and strong is where you are putting out a good effort (somewhere in the area of 75% to 80%) but surely, not going an all out sprint, type of fast. You will probably be able to feel the difference between a good strong swim vs. an easy swim that you would do when warming up or recovering after a particularly challenging set of swims.

Let us go through a typical workout together and make sure you are comfortable reading it and understand how to execute it. The information shown in parenthesis is for the sake of explanation and in most cases will not appear on a workout. In this sample, I included the "times" to use for intervals. Normally, these times will not appear because you will be determining your own interval time. On the workouts shown in the Beginner Workouts Chapter (10), these types of explanations will be included in most of the workouts. During any given workout, if you are swimming an interval or rest interval set, you know that your rest times are predetermined and very specific. Other than these interval sets, the rest you take between swims or sets of swims is at your discretion. As you progress, you will realize that you are requiring less rest time between swims.

In the chapter you are now reading, "All You Need To Know About Workouts", all of the information about executing the workouts has been covered, so I hope you do not mind the repetition of this material in the upcoming sample. Do not let this example intimidate you if you are a novice or beginner. The workouts in the "Beginner Workouts" chapter are easier, more instructive and lesser in total yardage.

Total Workout - 3,000 yards

WARM-UP = 800 yards, consisting of:
1x200 easy swim (swim an easy 200)
6x50 kick/swims (on each of the six 50s, kick the first 25 yards and swim back)
6x50 drill/swims. (on each of the six 50s, perform a drill going down the lane and swim the 25 yards coming back)

MAIN SET = 1950 yards consisting of:
4x100 rest interval (swim 4x100 (strong), 35 second rest between each 100)
1x100 easy pull (pull an easy 100, using a pull buoy)

8x50 interval* (8x50 leaving every 1 minute and 30 seconds)
*When the instruction is not specific as to swim, kick, pull etc. you always SWIM.

1x100 easy pull (use your pull buoy, with all pulls)

3x100 rest interval. (swim 3x100 (strong) with a 35-second rest between each 100)
1x100 easy pull

6x50 interval
1x100 easy pull

COOL DOWN = 250 yards, consisting of:
1x250 choice (Pull or swim any stroke of your choice, all easy, to cool down)

The next time a swim meet is available to watch on TV, (probably the 2008 Olympics) you will be eager to watch and will view it from a very different perspective. You will be checking out the almost flawless technique these amazing athletes display and will now fully appreciate the unbelievable speeds they attain. Notice that the swim time difference between the winner and even the fourth to sixth place finisher will most probably be less then a second. As a swimmer, you will learn or realize how precious five seconds can be. In a workout, when the interval time you chose is pushing and challenging you to the highest degree, a five-second increase in that time will make it an absolute breeze. When you rest between swim sets or within a set where you do not have to leave on a given interval, thirty seconds will start to feel like a long time and one minute an eternity. Believe me; you will get to that point.

A great question that must be addressed is—How do I remember the workout I chose to do, when I get to the pool? Here are some answers:

1 - Memorize it. Memorizing is not as difficult as it might sound since virtually all of the workouts follow some kind of a pattern. Once you spot the pattern, remembering, is easy.

2 - Make a copy and laminate it. A laminated copy will be water resistant and you can save it for future use.

3 - Make a copy and place it in a clear plastic sleeve. These sleeves are available at stationery stores.

3 - Make a copy on plain paper. At poolside, wet the paper and it will stick to the ledge of the pool that faces you when you are in the water. Please do not forget to remove the paper when you have finished your workout or it will eventually shred and create a mess.

SWIMMERS, TAKE YOUR MARKS, GET SET, GO!

That is how they **start** a race at a swim meet and now it is time to **start** your training program.

CHAPTER TEN

BEGINNER WORKOUTS

On your initial attempts at these workouts, if you cannot complete any of the swims as shown, stop and rest where necessary. In other words, if the first swim in the warm-up is 1x100 and after your first 25 or 50 yards, you are too tired to go on, simply stop, take the rest you need and then finish the required distance. Your endurance will gradually increase as you continue to do these routines.

WORKOUT #1 - 700 yards total distance

WARM-UP = 400 yards, consisting of:
1x100 easy swim (break this into two, 50 yard swims, if necessary)
6x50 with fins:
first 50, catch-up drill
second 50, finger tip drag drill
third 50, single arm swim drill
fourth 50, single arm drill with the other arm
fifth 50, brush your leg drill
sixth 50, fist drill

MAIN SET = 200 yards, consisting of:
4x50 rest interval (example: swim 4x50 with 30 seconds rest between each)

COOL DOWN - 1x100 easy pull

WORKOUT #2 total distance - 800 yards

WARM-UP = 400 yards, consisting of:
1x100 easy swim
6x50 with fins, kickboard optional. (each 50, kick 25 fast / 25 easy)

MAIN SET = 200 yards, consisting of:
8x25:
first 25, swim easy
second 25, build up (start easy and gradually get faster)
third 25, build down (start fast and gradually slow down)
fourth 25, swim fast
fifth 25, swim easy
sixth 25, swim moderate
seventh 25, swim strong
eighth 25, swim easy

COOL DOWN - 1x200 easy pull

WORKOUT #3 total distance - 850 yards

WARM-UP = 400 yards, consisting of:
1x100 easy swim
1x100 easy pull
4x50 drill/swims with fins (on ea.50, drill25 and swim25) use 4 different drills

MAIN SET = 250 yards, consisting of:
1x50 moderate speed swim
1x100 easy pull
1x100 moderate speed swim

COOL DOWN - 1x200 easy pull

WORKOUT #4 total distance - 950 yards

WARM-UP = 500 yards, consisting of:
1x100 easy swim
1x100 easy pull
1x100 with fins 7/3/7 drill
4x50 drill/swims with fins (drill 25 and swim 25 on each 50)

MAIN SET = 250 yards, consisting of:
1x25 easy swim
1x25 fast swim
1x50 easy swim
1x50 strong swim
1x100 easy swim

COOL DOWN - 1x200 easy pull

If you enjoyed the above and wish to convert it into a longer distance workout, you can repeat the 200-yard "main set" before continuing on to the "cool down". In making that change you will be altering the total distance to be 1,100 yards. Obviously, you can shorten the workout by eliminating any of the elements.

By applying this concept, you can change the total distance of any of the workouts.

WORKOUT #5 total distance - 1,150 yards

WARM-UP = 500 yards, consisting of:
1x100 easy swim
2x200 w/fins. (Each 200 is 1x50 kick, 1x50 swim, 1x50 drill, 1x50 swim)

MAIN SET = 450 yards, consisting of:
1x100 moderate swim
1x200 easy pull
1x150 moderate swim

COOL DOWN - 1x200 easy pull

WORKOUT #6 total distance - 1,000 yards

WARM-UP = 550 yards, consisting of:
1x150 easy swim
4x100 w/fins:
first 100, kick25 / swim75
second 100, kick50 / swim50
third 100, kick75 / swim25
fourth 100, kick100

MAIN SET = 350 yards, consisting of:
1x100 easy pull
5x50 (on each 50, swim 25 fast and 25 easy. Try to not take more then 30 seconds rest between each 50. Hopefully you will be recovering from the fast 25 when swimming the easy 25)

COOL DOWN - 1x100 easy pull

WORKOUT #7 total distance - 1200 yards

WARM-UP = 500 yards, consisting of:
1x100 Easy swim
3x100 w/fins:
1st 100, 1x25 kick / 1x75 drill
2nd 100, 1x50 kick / 1x50 drill
3rd 100, 1x75 kick / 1x25 drill
1x100 easy pull

MAIN SET = 600 yards, consisting of:
1x25 strong swim
1x50 easy swim
1x75 strong
1x100 easy pull
1x75 strong swim
1x50 easy swim
1x25 strong swim

4x50 - fast 50 / easy 50 / fast 50 / easy 50. (Take whatever rest time you require between each 50).

COOL DOWN - 1x100 easy pull

WORKOUT #8 total distance - 1,250 yards

WARM-UP = 750 yards, consisting of:
1x100 easy swim
1x100 easy pull
1x100 easy swim
6x75 with fins (each 75, kick25 / drill25 / swim25)

MAIN SET = 300 yards, consisting of:
3x100:
First 100, 75 easy / 25 fast (75 yards easy and 25 yards fast)
Second 100, 50 easy / 50 strong (50 yards easy and 50 yards strong)
Third 100, all moderate speed

COOL DOWN - 1x200 easy pull

WORKOUT #9 total distance - 1,000 yards

WARM-UP = 350 yards, consisting of:
1x50 easy swim
1x50 easy pull
1x50 easy swim
2x50 kick/swims w/fins (on each 50, kick 25/swim 25)
2x50 drill/swims w/fins (on each 50, drill 25/swim 25)

MAIN SET = 550 yards, consisting of:
4x50 on a rest interval (these 4 should be strong swims with a consistent rest time, between each. You pick the rest interval you can cope with. As a starting point, try for 20 to 30 seconds rest.)
1x50 easy pull
3x50 rest interval, as above.
1x50 easy pull
2x50 rest interval, as above.

COOL DOWN = 100 yards, consisting of:
1x50 easy pull
1x50 easy swim

WORKOUT #10 total distance - 1300 yards

WARM-UP = 500 yards, consisting of:
1x200 easy swim
3x100 w/fins:
1st 100, 25 drill/75 kick
2nd 100, 50 drill/50 kick
3rd 100, 75 drill/25 kick

MAIN SET = 700 yards, consisting of:
2x100 build (gradually increase your speed within ea.100 & rest between ea.100)
1x100 easy pull
4x50 build (gradually increase your speed within ea.50 & rest between ea.50)
1x200 easy pull

COOL DOWN - 1x100 easy swim

WORKOUT #11 total distance - 1,550 yards

WARM-UP = 650 yards, consisting of:
1x100 easy swim
1x100 easy pull
6x75 with fins. (Each 75, 25 left arm only drill/ 25 right arm only drill/ 25 swim)

MAIN SET = 700 yards, consisting of:
6x50 each 50 is 25fast/25easy (try not to rest between the fast & the easy 25)
1x200 easy pull
4x50 alternating, fast 50s and easy 50s (rest between 50s)

COOL DOWN - 1x200 easy pull

WORKOUT # 12 total distance - 1,800

WARM-UP = 600 yards, consisting of:
1x200 easy swim
4x100 KLRS with fins. 100 of KLRS =
Kick 25 yards
Left arm only drill, for 25 yards
Right arm only drill, for 25 yards
Swim 25 yards

MAIN SET = 1,000 yards, consisting of:
1x200 moderate swim
1x200 easy pull
1x100 fast swim
1x100 easy swim
3x50 descend (each 50 should be 2 to 5 seconds faster then the one before it. These are not intervals, so you may take whatever rest you need, between each 50).

1x150 easy pull
1x50 fast swim
1x50 easy pull

COOL DOWN - 1x200 of your choice)

* During the "fast" swims in the above workout, check your swim times on the pace clock. Knowing your times will be very helpful when, in later workouts, you will want to establish an interval time.

WORKOUT # 13 total distance - 1,950 yards

WARM-UP = 900 yards, consisting of:
1x300 easy pull
6x50 kick (use different kicks - two 50s each, of dolphin, freestyle and side kicking)
6x50 drill (use different drills)

MAIN SET = 950 yards, consisting of:
1x200 easy to moderate swim
1x300 easy pull
1x100 moderate swim
1x200 easy pull
1x50 fast swim
1x100 easy pull

COOL DOWN - 1x100 of your choice

WORKOUT #14 total distance - 1,700 yards

WARM-UP = 800 yards, consisting of:
1x100 easy swim
8x50 kick/drills w/fins (on each 50, kick25 / drill25)
1x100 kick w/fins (use different kicks within the 100)
1x100 drill w/fins (four different drills, 25 of each)
1x100 easy pull

MAIN SET = 800 yards, consisting of:
1x200 easy swim
1x100 moderate to strong swim
1x100 easy pull
1x50 fast swim
1x100 easy pull

1x100 easy swim
1x50 moderate to strong swim
1x50 easy pull
1x50 fast swim

COOL DOWN - 1x100 easy pull

WORKOUT #15 total distance - 2,000 yards

WARM-UP = 600 yards, consisting of:
1x100 easy swim
1x100 easy pull
4x100 KLRS w/fins (check Workout #12, if you do not remember KLRS)

MAIN SET = 1,300 yards, consisting of:
4x150:
1st 150, build
2nd 150, easy
3rd 150, strong
4th 150, easy pull

4x100:
1st 100, build
2nd 100, easy
3rd 100, strong
4th 100, easy pull

4x50:
1st 50, build
2nd 50, easy
3rd 50, fast
4th 50, easy pull

4x25:
1st 25, build
2nd 25, easy
3rd 25 fast
4th 25, easy pull

COOL DOWN - 1x100 choice

WORKOUT #16 total distance - 1,600 yards

WARM-UP = 700 yards, consisting of:
1x100 easy swim
2x50 kick (use 2 different kicks, 50 of each)
1x100 drill (mix up drills within the 100)
2x100 kick (all freestyle kick, 100 moderate / 100 easy)
1x200 drill (4 different drills, 50 yards of each)

MAIN SET = 800 yards, consisting of:
4x50 interval (see below to review establishing interval time)
1x100 easy pull

3x50 interval
1x150 easy pull

2x50 interval
1x100 easy pull

COOL DOWN - 1x100 of your choice

Being that WORKOUT #16 was the first to contain "intervals," let us take some time to, once again, review what these intervals are, and how to go about determining your own interval time.

Intervals are a given number of repeat swims, of a specific distance, swam at a determined departure time. Example, 4x50 on 1:30, means that you will execute four 50-yard swims, leaving every one minute and 30 seconds.

Next step is to determine your interval time. Swim 50 yards at about 80% effort and check your swim time on the pace clock. For the sake of this example, let us say that you swam that 50, in one minute and ten seconds. Factoring in about 20 seconds rest, your interval time would become 1:30 (one minute and thirty seconds). Therefore, you are going to leave every 1:30.

If, after going through the suggested steps to determine an interval, you find that the interval time you set for yourself is too challenging or too easy, adjust accordingly.

Please do not stop doing your workouts because you are having a difficult time with the concept of determining and performing intervals. Until you "get it", when a workout calls for "intervals", use "rest intervals". In the above example of 4x50 on an interval, make it a "rest interval" by simply swimming each 50 at about 80% effort, determine a rest time you require between each swim and keep that rest time, constant. For instance, you could swim 4x50 with 20 seconds rest between each 50.

If, after completing the workouts in this chapter, you feel that you are ready to advance, you may begin to experiment with the workouts in the next chapter, which are a step up in degree of difficulty. If you do not feel you are ready, or if after trying a couple of Chapter 11 workouts, you think that they are still a bit too challenging, go back to the beginner workouts and repeat them as they are, or begin to add some additional distance to each one. To add some yardage to a workout simply repeat one or more sets contained in the "main set" before proceeding to the "cool down".

CHAPTER ELEVEN

MY FAVORITE WORKOUTS

In the first few workouts shown in this chapter, I will try to explain, in parenthesis, most of the terms and vernacular used. Eventually, those types of explanations will not appear. If you get to a workout that reads 4x50 kick/swims and you do not remember what a kick/swim is, please check Chapter10, ALL YOU NEED TO KNOW ABOUT WORKOUTS, and you will find that type of information. In a short period of time, this will all become very familiar to you and there will no longer be a need to check back.

Each workout in this chapter has an "A" and a "B" version. Both workouts will be of the same concept or style. The "A" will usually consist of a total of 2,000 yards. The "B" version will consist of approximately 3,000 yards, and in addition, will be a more challenging workout. If you are a true novice, you probably should not attempt to perform WORKOUT #1A and then go directly to #1B. You will be better served to advance to WORKOUT #2A then #3A and so forth. The next logical step would be to add some distance to the "A" workouts by repeating one of the sets in the "main set" before going on to the "cool down". When you feel you are ready, start to experiment with some of the more challenging "B", versions. Remember that you can alter the distance of any workout by repeating or deleting sets from the "main set" and you are the one determining your speeds and interval times. These options are allowing you to tailor each of the workouts to your present abilities.

I know you cannot wait to get started but I wanted to convey two random workout tips that I thought of while swimming this morning:

1 - Stay in the moment. Concentrate on the set of swims you are working on. This applies, if you are in an easy warm-up swim or if in a tough portion of the main set. Do not start thinking, positively or negatively about the next set you are required to swim and above all, do not let your mind wander aimlessly. Remain attentive to what you are attempting to accomplish at all times.

2 - When in the midst of a very challenging set, you are beginning to think about how tired you are becoming, start to focus on some parts of your technique. We all know how mental these types of workouts are and simply switching your focus from thoughts of fatigue to those of efficiency, will do wonders. Go through a personal checklist of two or three of the techniques you know unravel when you are attempting to swim fast as oxygen debt is setting in. Think about them and concentrate on performing them properly. This method really works, folks. It is amazing how fast thoughts of what appear to be total exhaustion, are dismissed from your mind.

When I am in this situation, the very first thing I think of is to make sure I am breathing out forcefully. Next on my checklist is allowing only one side of my goggle to clear the water when inhaling which keeps my head down and insures proper body balance. Number three on my personal list is to concentrate on good body rotation as my arms are extending forward on their glide.

That does it for me, now you find what works for you and be ready with your checklist.

WORKOUT#1A total distance 2,000 yards

WARM-UP = 600 yards, consisting of:
1x200 easy swim
4x50 kick on your side w/fins (each 50, 25 on left side/25 on your right side)
1x100 catch-up drill w/fins
1x100 1-arm swimming drill w/fins (switch arms every 25)

MAIN SET = 1,200 yards, consisting of:
1x200 easy to moderate swim
4x50 rest interval
1x200 easy pull

1x200 easy to moderate swim
8x25 alternating, fast 25/easy 25
1x200 easy pull

COOL DOWN - 1x200 choice

WORKOUT #1B total distance - 3,000 yards

WARM-UP = 1,100 yards, consisting of:
1x400 easy swim
6x50 kick on your side w/fins (each 50, 25 on your left side/25 on your right)
8x50 drill w/fins (alternating, catch-up & acceleration drills)

MAIN SET = 1,800 yards, consisting of:
1x200 easy to moderate swim
2x100 descend
1x200 easy pull

1x200 (descend the above 1x200 easy to moderate swim)
4x50 on an interval time
1x200 easy pull

1x200 moderate swim
8x25 alternating, fast 25/easy 25
1x200 easy pull

COOL DOWN - 1x100 choice

WORKOUT #2A total distance - 2,000 yards

WARM-UP = 900 yards, consisting of:
1x300 easy swim
1x100 kick w/fins, kickboard optional
1x100 drill w/fins (four different drills, 25 yds. of each drill)
Repeat the above 1x100 kick & 1x100 drill, **2** more times.

MAIN SET = 800 yards, consisting of:
1x200 easy swim or pull
4x50 rest interval (example: 2x50 @ 80% effort with 30 seconds rest between 50s)
1x100 easy swim or pull
3x50 rest interval
1x50 easy swim
2x50 rest interval

COOL DOWN - 1x300 easy pull

WORKOUT # 2B total distance - 3,000 yards

WARM-UP = 900 yards, consisting of:
1x300 easy swim
1x100 kick w/fins, kickboard optional
1x100 drill w/fins (four different drills, 25 of each drill)
Repeat the above 1x100 kick & 1x100 drill, **2** more times

MAIN SET = 1,700 yards, consisting of:
1x400 easy swim
5x50 on an interval (example: 2x50 leaving on 1:30)
1x300 easy swim
4x50 on an interval

1x200 easy swim
3x50 on an interval

1x100 easy swim
2x50 on an interval

COOL DOWN - 1x400 easy pull

WORKOUT#3A total distance - 2,000 yards

WARM-UP = 800 yards, consisting of:
1x200 easy swim
6x50 kick/swims w/fins (kick 25, swim 25 –use different kicks)
6x50 drill/swims w/fins (drill 25, swim 25 - use different drills)

MAIN SET = 1,200 yards, consisting of:
1x50 build (gradually increase your speed within the 50)
1x50 easy
1x50 fast
1x150 easy pull
Repeat above 300

1x25 build
1x25 easy
1x50 fast
1x100 easy pull
Repeat above 200 set, **2** more times (600 yards)

WORKOUT #3B total distance - 3,000 yards

WARM-UP = 800 yards, consisting of:
1x200 easy swim
6x50 kick/swims with fins (kick 25, swim 25 - use different kicks)
6x50 drill/swims with fins (drill 25, swim 25 - use different drills)

MAIN SET = 2,000 yards, consisting of:
1x100 build (gradually increase your speed within the 100)
1x100 easy
1x100 fast
1x300 easy pull
Repeat above 600
1x50 build (gradually increase your speed within the 50)
1x50 easy
1x50 fast
1x150 easy pull
Repeat above 300

1x25 build
1x25 easy
1x50 fast
1x100 pull

COOL DOWN - 1x200 choice

WORKOUT #4A total distance - 2,050 yards

WARM-UP = 600 yards, consisting of:
1x200 easy swim
Kick the below 400 yd. pyramid with fins (freestyle kick for all of these)
25 fast
50 easy
75 fast
100 easy
75 fast
50 easy
25 fast

MAIN SET = 1,350 yards, consisting of:
2x100 descend (second 100 a few seconds faster then the first)
1x100 easy pull
Repeat above 300 yd. set

3x50 descend (each 50 a few seconds faster then the one before)
1x100 easy pull
Repeat above 250 yd. set **2** more times (total, 750 yds.)

COOL DOWN - 1x100 easy swim or pull

WORKOUT #4B total distance - 3,000 yards

WARM-UP = 600 yards
SAME WARM-UP AS ABOVE (#4A)

MAIN SET = 2,200 yards, consisting of:
2x100 descend
1x100 easy pull
Repeat above 300 yd. set **3** more times. (total, 1,200 yds.)

3x50 descend
1x100 easy pull
Repeat above 250 yd. set, **3** more times. (total, 1,000 yds.)

COOL DOWN - 200 yards of your choice (any stroke, w/without fins or pull buoy)

WORKOUT #5A total distance - 2,000 yards

WARM-UP = 600 yards, consisting of:
1x200 easy swim
1x50 kick, 1x50 drill, 1x50 swim. w/fins
Repeat 1x50 kick, 1x50 drill, 1x50 swim. w/fins
1x100 easy pull

MAIN SET = 1,200 yards, consisting of:
3x100:
1st 100, (25 fast, 75 easy)
2nd 100, (50 fast, 50 easy)
3rd100, (easy)

5x50 rest interval
1x50 easy pull
5x50 rest interval
1x50 easy pull

12x25 (alternate fast 25s and easy 25s)

COOL DOWN - 1x200 easy pull or swim or 100 of each

WORKOUT #5B total distance - 3,000 yards

WARM-UP - 600 yards, same as above (#5A)

MAIN SET = 2,200 yards, consisting of:
4x100:
1st 100, (75 fast, 25 easy)
2nd 100, (50 fast, 50 easy)
3rd 100, (25 fast, 75 easy)
4th 100, (fast)

1x400 easy to moderate
4x100 on an interval
1x200 easy pull
6x50 on an interval
1x100 easy pull

16x25 (alternate fast 25s and easy 25)

COOL DOWN - 1x200 easy pull or swim or 100 of each

WORKOUT #6A total distance - 2,000 yards

WARM-UP = 500 yards, consisting of:
1x300 easy swim (or 1x100 swim, 1x100 pull, and 1x100 swim)
4x50 drills with fins (4 different drills, 50 yds. of each)

MAIN SET = 1,400 yards, consisting of:
1x25 fast / 1x25 easy

1x50 fast / 1x50 easy pull

1x100 strong / 1x100 easy pull

1x100 fast / 1x100 easy pull

1x50 fast / 1x50 easy pull

1x25 fast / 1x25 easy
Repeat above 700 yard set

COOL DOWN - 1x100 your choice

WORKOUT #6B total distance - 3,000 yards

WARM-UP = 500 yards. Same as above (#6A)

MAIN SET = 2,400 yards, consisting of:
1x100 fast
1x100 easy pull

1x200 fast
1x200 easy pull

1x300 fast
1x300 easy pull
Repeat the 300 fast & 300 easy pull

1x200 fast
1x200 easy pull

1x100 fast
1x100 easy pull

COOL DOWN - 1x100 your choice

WORKOUT #7A total distance - 2,000 yards

WARM-UP = 800 yards, consisting of:
1x200 easy swim
3x200 w/fins (each 200 consists of 100 kick/100 drill)

MAIN SET = 1,000 yards, consisting of:
3x50 descend
1x100 easy pull
Repeat above 250 set

2x50 (alternate a fast 50/easy 50)
1x100 easy pull
Repeat above 200 set

4x25 (alternating, fast 25s/easy 25s)

COOL DOWN - 1x200 choice

WORKOUT #7B total distance - 3,100 yards

WARM-UP = 800 yards, consisting of:
1x200 easy swim
3x200 w/fins (each 200 consists of 100 kick/100 drill)

MAIN SET = 2,100 yards, consisting of:
3x100 descend
1x100 easy pull

3x50 descend
1x100 easy pull
Repeat above 650 set

4x100 (alternating, fast 100s and easy 100s)
1x100 easy pull

4x50 (alternating, fast 50s and easy 50s)
1x100 easy pull

COOL DOWN - 1x200 choice

WORKOUT # 8A total distance - 2000 yards

WARM-UP = 800 yards, consisting of:
1x200 easy swim

1x25 kick with fins
1x50 drill with fins
1x25 swim with fins
Repeat the above 100 yd. kick, drill, swim w/fins set, **5** more times (600 yds. total)

MAIN SET = 1,050 yards, consisting of:
1x200 easy swim
4x50 rest interval
1x100 easy pull

1x100 easy to moderate swim
3x50 rest interval
1x100 easy pull

1x100 easy to moderate swim
2x50 try a swim interval rather than a rest interval

COOL DOWN - 1x150 easy pull or swim

WORKOUT #8B total distance - 3,000 yards

WARM-UP = 800 yards same as above (#8A)

MAIN SET = 2,000 yards, consisting of:
1x400 easy
8x50 on an interval
1x100 easy pull

1x300 easy
6x50 on an interval
1x100 easy pull

1x200 easy
4x50 on an interval

COOL DOWN - 1x200 choice

WORKOUT #9A total distance - 2,000 yards

WARM-UP = 500 yards, consisting of:
1x200 easy swim
2x50 kick/swims with fins
4x50 drill/swims with fins

MAIN SET = 1,200 yards, consisting of:
1x300 easy pull
3x100 rest interval

1x300 easy pull
6x50 rest interval

COOL DOWN = 300 yards (choice)

WORKOUT #9B total distance 3,000 yards

WARM-UP = 500 yards same as above (#9A)

MAIN SET = 2,350 yards, consisting of:
1x300 easy pull
2x200 descend

1x300 easy pull
3x100 on an interval

1x300 easy pull
6x50 on an interval

1x300 easy pull
3x50 descend

COOL DOWN - 1x150 choice

WORKOUT #10A total distance - 2,000 yards

WARM-UP = 900 yards, consisting of:
1x100 easy swim

1x50 catch-up drill w/fins
1x50 1 arm swimming drill w/fins
1x50 acceleration drill w/fins
1x50 fingertip drag drill w/fins
Repeat the above drills, **3** more times

MAIN SET = 1,000 yards, consisting of:
4x100 (alternating, swim100/ pull100. Swims should be strong &
pulls are easy)

8x50 (alternate swims and pulls as above)

4x50 on an interval

COOL DOWN - 1x100 choice

WORKOUT #10B total distance - 3,000 yards

WARM-UP = 900 yards same as above (#10A)

MAIN SET = 1,900 yards, consisting of:
10x100 (alternating 100 yd. swims & 100 yd. pulls. Swims 80% effort, pulls are easy.)
There should not be much resting in the 10x100 set above or the 10x50 set below. Take the least amount of rest as possible after the strong (85% effort) swims. Recovery will come with the easy pulls. After the easy pulls, there will not be much rest necessary. Try 30 to 45 seconds after strong swims and 20 seconds after the pulls, and then adjust to your ability.

10x50 (alternating swims & pulls, as above.)

4x100 HYPOXIC pulling (use a 5, 2, 4, 3 breathing pattern).
During each 100,
on the first 25, breathe every 5th stroke,
on the second 25, breathe every 2nd stroke,
on the third 25 breathe every 4th stroke,
and on the last 25, breathe every 3rd stroke)

COOL DOWN - 1x200 easy swim

WORKOUT #11A total distance - 2,000 yards

WARM-UP = 500 yards, consisting of:
1x200 easy swim
3x100 KLRS with fins 100 of KLRS = Kick, 25 yds.
Left arm only drill, 25yds.
Right arm only drill, 25 yds.
Swim, 25 yds.

MAIN SET = 1,350 yards, consisting of:
1x100 easy swim
1x100 strong swim
1x100 easy pull
Repeat this set **2** more times

1x50 easy swim
1x50 fast
1x50 easy pull
Repeat this set **2** more times

COOL DOWN - 1x150 choice

WORKOUT #11B total distance - 3,000 yards

WARM-UP = 900 yards, consisting of:
1x300 easy swim
4x100 KLRS (see above, #11A for explanation of KLRS)
1x200 easy pull

MAIN SET = 1,950 yards, consisting of:
1x300 easy swim
1x300 strong swim
1x300 easy pull

1x200 easy to moderate swim
1x200 fast swim
1x200 easy pull

1x100 moderate
1x100 fast
1x100 easy pull

1x50 moderate
1x50 fast
1x50 easy pull

COOL DOWN - 1x150 choice

WORKOUT #12A total distance - 1,950 yards

WARM-UP = 1,050 yards, consisting of:
1x200 easy swim

1x25 catch-up drill w/fins
1x25 fingertip drag drill w/fins
1x25 brush your leg drill w/fins
Repeat the above drills, **5** more times

2x100 freestyle kick w/fins, (1st 100 fast / 2nd 100 easy)

2x50 freestyle kick w/fins, (1st 50 fast / 2nd 50 easy)

1x100 freestyle kick w/fins all easy

MAIN SET = 700 yards, consisting of:
4x50 rest interval
1x50 easy pull

3x50 rest interval
1x50 easy pull

2x50 rest interval
1x50 easy pull

1x50 fast
1x50 easy pull

COOL DOWN - 1x200 easy pull

WORKOUT #12B total distance - 3,000 yards

WARM-UP = 1,100 yards, consisting of:
1x200 easy swim

4x75 drills w/fins (Each 75 - the 1st 25 is catch-up, 2nd 25 is fingertip drag, 3rd 25 is fist drill)

2x150 freestyle kick w/fins (1st 150 is fast, 2nd 150 is easy)

2x100 freestyle kick w/fins (1st 100 is fast, 2nd 100 is easy)

2x50 freestyle kick w/fins (1st 50 is fast, 2nd 50 is easy)

MAIN SET = 1,700 yards, consisting of:
5x50 interval
1x250 easy swim

4x50 interval
1x200 easy swim

3x50 interval
1x150 easy swim

2x50 interval
1x100 easy swim

3x100 pull (2nd 100 use a 5,2,4,3 hypoxic breathing pattern)

COOL DOWN - 1x200 easy swim

WORKOUT #13A total distance - 2,000 yards

WARM-UP = 400 yards, consisting of:
1x100 easy swim
4x75 w/fins (each 75 consists of 25 kick, 25 drill & 25 swim)

MAIN SET = 1,500 yards, consisting of:
1x200 easy swim
2x100 rest interval
1x100 easy pull

1x100 easy swim
2x50 try a regular interval rather than a rest interval
1x100 easy pull
Repeat this 300 yd. set

1x50 easy swim
1x50 fast
1x100 easy pull
Repeat this 200 yd. set

COOL DOWN - 100 choice

WORKOUT #13B total distance - 3,000 yards

WARM-UP = 500 yards, consisting of:
1x200 easy swim
4x75 w/fins (each 75 consists of 25 kick, 25 drill & 25 swim)

MAIN SET = 2,300 yards, consisting of:
1x400 easy
4x100 on an interval
1x100 easy pull

1x400 easy
8x50 on an interval
1x100 easy pull

1x400 easy
1x100 fast

COOL DOWN - 1x200 easy pull

WORKOUT #14A total distance - 2,000 yards

WARM-UP = 900 yards, consisting of:
1x100 easy swim
1x100 easy pull
1x100 easy swim
6x50 kick/swims w/fins
6x50 drill/swims w/fins

MAIN SET = 950 yards, consisting of:
1x200 moderate swim (check your 200 time)
1x300 easy pull

1x100 moderate to fast swim (check your 100 time)
1x200 easy swim

1x50 fast (check your 50 time)
1x100 easy pull

COOL DOWN - 1x150 choice

WORKOUT #14B total distance - 3,000 yards

WARM-UP = 900 yards, consisting of:
1x300 easy swim
6x50 kick/swims w/fins
6x50 drill/swims w/fins

MAIN SET = 2,100 yards, consisting of:
1x400 easy to moderate
1x500 easy pull

1x300 moderate
1x400 easy pull

1x200 moderate to fast
1x300 easy pull

WORKOUT #15A total distance - 2,000 yards

WARM-UP = 550 yards, consisting of:
1x150 easy swim
4x100 KLRS w/fins (Kick, Left, Right, Swim. 25 of each =100)

MAIN SET = 1,250 yards, consisting of:
1x100 easy swim
5x50 rest interval

1x100 easy swim or pull
4x50 rest interval

1x100 easy swim or pull
3x50 rest interval

1x100 easy swim or pull
2x50 rest interval

1x100 easy swim or pull
1x50 fast

COOL DOWN - 1x200 choice

WORKOUT #15B total distance - 3,050 yards

WARM-UP = 600 yards, consisting of:
1x200 easy swim
4x100 KLRS w/fins

MAIN SET = 2,250 yards, consisting of:
1x100 easy swim
8x50 on an interval

1x100 easy swim or pull
7x50 on an interval

1x100 easy swim or pull
6x50 on an interval

1x100 easy swim or pull
5x50 on an interval

1x100 easy swim or pull
4x50 on an interval

1x100 easy swim or pull
3x50 on an interval

COOL DOWN - 1x200 choice

WORKOUT #16A total distance - 2,150 yards

WARM-UP = 600 yards, consisting of:
1x100 easy swim
1x200 easy pull
6x50 kick/drills w/fins (kick down 25 and drill back 25)

MAIN SET = 1,350 yards

(SKIP stands for Swim, Kick, Interval, Pull)

Complete **3** SKIP sets as follows:

1x100 Swim (easy)
1x100 Kick (easy - fins and/or kickboard optional)
3x50 Interval
1x100 Pull (easy)
(Each SKIP set is 450 yards)

COOL DOWN - 1x200 easy pull

WORKOUT #16B total distance - 3,000 yards

WARM UP = 900 yards, consisting of:
1x400 easy swim
2x50 kick/swims w/fins
2x50 drill/swims w/fins
6x50 kick/drills w/fins

MAIN SET = 2,000 yards

(SKIP stands for Swim, Kick, Interval, Pull)

Complete **4** SKIP sets as follows:

1x100 Swim (easy)
1x100 Kick (easy - fins and/or kickboard optional)
4x50 Interval
1x100 Pull (easy)
(Each SKIP set is 500 yards)

COOL DOWN - 1x100 choice

WORKOUT #17A total distance - 2,100 yards

WARM-UP = 600 yards, consisting of:
1x100 easy swim
1x100 easy pull
1x100 easy swim
6x50 w/fins (alternate 50s. 50 drill / 50 swim)

MAIN SET = 1,400 yards, consisting of:
3x100 build (build each 100 & rest between each 100)
1x100 easy pull

4x50 on an interval or rest interval
1x100 easy pull

Repeat the above 700 yards

COOL DOWN - 1x100 easy swim

WORKOUT #17B total distance - 3,100 yards

WARM-UP = 900 yards, consisting of:
1x300 easy swim
6x50 w/fins (alternate 50s. drill 50 / swim 50)
6x50 each 50 = fast 25 / easy 25

MAIN SET = 2,000 yards, consisting of:
4x100 build (build each 100 & rest between each 100)
1x200 easy pull

6x50 on an interval
1x100 easy pull

Repeat the above 1,000 yards

COOL DOWN - 1x200 easy swim or pull

WORKOUT #18A total distance - 2,100 yards

WARM-UP = 500 yards, consisting of:
1x100 easy swim
4x50 kick/swims w/fins
4x50 drill/swims w/fins

MAIN SET = 1,450 yards, consisting of:
1x300 easy pull or swim
4x50 on an interval or rest interval

1x200 easy pull or swim
4x50 on an interval or rest interval

1x100 easy pull or swim
4x50 on an interval or rest interval

1x50 easy pull or swim
4x50 on an interval or rest interval

COOL DOWN - 1x150 choice

WORKOUT #18B total distance - 3,050 yards

WARM-UP = 800 yards, consisting of:
1x200 easy swim
6x50 kick/swims w/fins
6x50 drill/swims w/fins

MAIN SET = 2,050 yards, consisting of:
1x400 easy
4x50 on an interval

1x300 easy
4x50 on an interval

1x200 easy
4x50 on an interval

1x100 easy
4x50 on an interval

1x50 easy
4x50 on an interval

COOL DOWN - 1x200 easy pull

WORKOUT #19A total distance - 2,000 yards

WARM-UP = 900 yards, consisting of:
1x100 easy swim
1x200 easy pull
1x100 easy swim
1x100 7/3/7 drill, w/fins
8x50 w/fins (alternate 50 drill / 50 kick)

MAIN SET = 900 yards, consisting of:
1x50 easy
1x25 fast
1x50 easy
1x50 fast
1x50 easy
1x75 fast
1x50 easy
1x100 fast

Repeat 1x50 easy/1x100 fast

1x50 easy/1x75 fast
1x50easy/1x50 fast
1x50 easy/1x25 fast

COOL DOWN - 1x200 easy pull

WORKOUT #19B total distance - 3,000 yards

WARM-UP = 1,000 yards, consisting of:
1x400 easy swim
1x200 7/3/7 drill w/fins
8x50 w/fins alternate 50s (kick 50 / drill 50)

MAIN SET = 1,800 yards, consisting of:
1x50 easy
1x25 fast
1x50 easy
1x50 fast
1x50 easy
1x75 fast
1x50 easy
1x100 fast
1x50 easy
1x200 fast

Repeat 1x50easy/1x200fast, and then go back up.

1x50easy/1x100fast
1x50easy/1x75fast
1x50easy/1x50fast
1x50easy/1x25fast

COOL DOWN - 1x200 choice

WORKOUT #20A total distance - 2,100 yards

WARM-UP = 800 yards, consisting of:
1x200 easy swim
6x50 freestyle kick w/fins (25 fast / 25 easy on each 50)
6x50 drills w/fins (use some different drills)

MAIN SET = 1,200 yards, consisting of:
1x200 easy swim
4x50 on an interval

1x100 easy swim
2x50 on an interval
PULL the above 600 yd. set. (try to hold your normal interval time when pulling)

COOL DOWN - 1x100 easy swim

WORKOUT #20B total distance - 3,100 yards

WARM-UP = 900 yards, consisting of:
1x300 easy swim
6x50 freestyle kick w/fins (alternating fast 50 / easy 50)
6x50 drills w/fins (use some different drills)

MAIN SET = 2,000 yards, consisting of:
1x300 easy to moderate
3x100 on an interval
1x100 easy pull

1x300 easy to moderate
3x100 descend
1x100 easy pull

1x300 easy to moderate
6x50 on an interval

COOL DOWN - 1x200 easy pull

WORKOUT #21A total distance - 2,000 yards

WARM-UP = 850 yards, consisting of:
1x100 easy swim
3x250 w/fins (on each 250, kick75/ swim75/ drill100)

MAIN SET = 1,050 yards, consisting of:
1x100 build
1x100 easy
1x100 fast

1x50 build
1x50 easy
1x50 fast

1x25 build
1x25 easy
1x25 fast

Repeat the above 3 sets, **Pulling**

COOL DOWN - 1x100 choice

WORKOUT #21B total distance - 3,000 yards

WARM-UP = 700 yards, consisting of:
1x300 easy swim
4x100 w/fins (on each 100, kick25/ swim25/ drill50)

MAIN SET = 2,100 yards, consisting of:
1x200 build
1x200 easy
1x200 fast

1x100 build
1x100 easy
1x100 fast

1x50 build
1x50 easy
1x50 fast

Repeat the above 3 sets, **Pulling**.

COOL DOWN - 1x200 choice

WORKOUT #22A total distance - 2,100 yards

WARM-UP = 700 yards, consisting of:
1x100 easy swim
1x100 easy pull
5x50 freestyle kick w/fins (keep alternating, 50 easy / 50 fast)
5x50 drill/swims w/fins

MAIN SET = 1,200 yards, consisting of:
1x100 easy swim or pull
2x50 on an interval

1x200 easy swim or pull
4x50 on an interval

1x200 easy swim or pull
4x50 on an interval

1x100 easy swim or pull
2x50 on an interval

COOL DOWN = 1x200 choice

WORKOUT #22B total distance = 3,100 yards

WARM-UP = 600 yards, consisting of:
1x200 easy swim
4x50 freestyle kick w/fins (keep alternating 50easy / 50 fast)
4x50 drill/swims w/fins

MAIN SET = 2,400 yards, consisting of:
1x100 easy swim
2x50 on an interval

1x200 easy swim or pull
4x50 on an interval

1x300 easy swim or pull
6x50 on an interval

1x300 easy swim or pull
6x50 on an interval

1x200 easy swim or pull
4x50 on an interval

1x100 easy swim or pull
2x50 on an interval

COOL DOWN - 1x100 choice

WORKOUT #23A total distance - 2,000 yards

WARM-UP = 600 yards, consisting of:
1x200 easy swim
4x50 (face the wall and hold on w/outstretched arms. Kick fast for 30 seconds & then immediately sprint 25. As soon as you arrive at the other end, grab the wall & kick fast for 30 seconds and then sprint back. Take a small break between each 50) The sprints are very fast swims. Fins are optional.
2x100 KLRS w/fins

MAIN SET = 1,200 yards, consisting of:
1x200 easy pull
1x100 strong
Repeat this 300 yd. set

1x100 easy pull
1x50 strong
Repeat this 150 yard set, **3** more times

COOL DOWN - 1x200 easy pull

WORKOUT #23B total distance - 3,100 yards

WARM-UP = 800 yards, consisting of:
1x300 easy swim
4x50 wall kick & sprint (see warm-up on workout #49A, for instructions)
3x100 KLRS w/fins

MAIN SET = 2,100 yards, consisting of:
1x200 easy swim or pull
1x100 fast
Repeat this 300 yd. set, **4** more times (1,500 yds. total)

1x100 easy swim or pull
1x50 fast
Repeat this 150 yd. set, **3** more times (600 yds. total)

COOL DOWN - 1x200 choice

WORKOUT #24A total distance - 2,000 yards

WARM-UP = 900 yards, consisting of:
1x200 easy swim
1x100 easy pull
1x200 easy swim
8x50 kick/drills w/fins

MAIN SET = 1,000 yards, consisting of:
3x50 descend
1x100 easy pull

3x50 on an interval
1x100 easy pull

3x50 descend
1x100 easy pull

3x50 on an interval
1x100 easy pull

COOL DOWN - 1x100 choice

WORKOUT #24B total distance - 3,100 yards

WARM-UP = 400 yards, consisting of:
1x200 easy swim
4x50 kick/drills w/fins

MAIN SET = 2,500 yards, consisting of:
3x100 descend
1x200 easy pull
Repeat the above 500 set, **2** more times. (total of 1,500 yards)

3x50 descend
1x100 easy pull
Repeat the above 250 set, **3** more times. (total of 1,000 yards)

COOL DOWN - 1x200 choice

WORKOUT #25A total distance - 2,000 yards

WARM-UP = 700 yards, consisting of:
1x200 easy swim
1x100 easy pull
4x100 KLRS w/fins (Kick, Left arm, Right arm, Swim. 25 of each = 100)

MAIN SET = 1,200 yards, consisting of:
6x200:
1st & 2nd 200 - 100 fast / 100 easy

3rd & 4th 200 - 75 fast/125 easy

5th & 6th 200 - 50 fast / 150 easy
Do not stop between the fast and easy portion of each 200-yard swim.

These are not intervals; take the rest you need between each of the 200-yard swims.

COOL DOWN - 1x100 choice

WORKOUT #25B total distance - 3,100 yards

WARM-UP = 500 yards, consisting of:
1x200 easy swim
3x100 KLRS w/fins

MAIN SET = 2,400 yards, consisting of:
5x400 & 4x100 pulls:
1st 400 moderate to strong swim
1x100 easy pull

2nd 400 - 200 fast / 200 easy
1x100 easy pull

3rd 400 - 50 fast / 150 easy / 50 fast / 150 easy
1x100 easy pull

4th 400 - 100 fast / 100 easy / 100 fast / 100 easy
1x100 easy pull

5th 400 - 150 fast / 50 easy / 150 fast / 50 easy

COOL DOWN - 1x200 choice

WORKOUT#26A total distance - 2,000 yards

WARM-UP = 1,000 yards, consisting of:
1x200 easy swim
1x200 easy pull
1x100 easy swim
5x100 w/fins (each 100, 75 drill/25 kick)

MAIN SET = 850 yards, consisting of:
2x100 rest interval
1x50 easy pull

3x50 on an interval
1x50 easy pull

1x100 strong
1x50 easy pull

4x50 on an interval
1x50 easy pull

COOL DOWN - 1x150 choice

WORKOUT #26B total distance - 3,100 yards

WARM-UP = 800 yards, consisting of:
1x300 easy swim
5x100 w/fins (each 100, 75 kick/25 drill)

MAIN SET = 2,100 yards, consisting of:
4x100 on an interval
1x50 easy pull

2x50 on an interval
1x50 easy pull

3x100 on an interval
1x50 easy pull

3x50 on an interval
1x50 easy pull

2x100 on an interval
1x50 easy pull

4x50 on an interval
1x50 easy pull

1x100 fast
1x50 easy pull

5x50 on an interval
1x50 easy pull

COOL DOWN - 1x200 choice

WORKOUT #27A total distance - 2,050 yards

WARM-UP = 500 yards, consisting of:
1x200 easy swim
6x50 kick w/fins (25 fast/25 easy on each 50)

MAIN SET = 1,350 yards

Complete **3** SKIP sets, as follows:

1x100 Swim easy
1x100 Kick (easy - fins and/or kickboard optional)
3x50 Interval
1x100 Pull easy

(each SKIP set is 450 yards)

COOL DOWN - 1x200 choice

WORKOUT #27B total distance - 3,100 yards

WARM-UP = 500 yards, consisting of:
1x200 easy swim
6x50 kick w/fins (25 fast/25 easy on each 50)

MAIN SET = 2,400 yards, consisting of:

Complete **4** SKIP sets, as follows:

1x100 Swim easy
1x100 Kick (easy - fins and/or kickboard optional)
6x50 Interval
1x100 Pull easy

(each SKIP set is 600 yards)

COOL DOWN - 1x200 choice

WORKOUT#28A total distance - 2,000 yards

WARM-UP = 700 yards, consisting of:
1x200 easy swim
1x100 easy pull
2x200 (ea. 200 consists of 50 kick/50 swim/50 drill/50/swim)

MAIN SET = 1,100 yards, consisting of:
4x100:
1st 100, 25 easy/25 fast/50 easy

2nd 100, fast

3rd 100, 25 easy/25 strong/50 fast

4th 100, easy

4x50:
1st 50, 25 fast/25 easy

2nd 50, fast

3rd 50, 25 easy/25 fast

4th 50, easy
Repeat above 4x50 set

3x100 pull (2nd 100 use an hypoxic breathing pattern)

COOL DOWN = 1x200 choice

WORKOUT #28B total distance - 3,000 yards

WARM-UP = 800 yards, consisting of:
1x400 easy swim
2x200 w/fins (ea. 200 consists of 50 kick/5o swim/50 drill/50 swim)

MAIN SET = 2,000 yards, consisting of:
4x200:
1st 200, 50 easy/50 fast/100 easy
2nd 200, fast
3rd 200, 50 fast/50 easy/100 fast
4th 200, easy

4x100:
1st 100, 25 easy/25 fast/50 easy
2nd 100, fast
3rd 100, 25 fast/25 easy/50 fast
4th 100, easy
Repeat the 4x100 set

4x50:
1st 50, 25 fast/25 easy
2nd 50, fast
3rd 50, 25 easy/25 fast
4th 50, easy

1x200 hypoxic pull (7,2,5,4 breathing pattern, 50 yds. of each)

COOL DOWN - 1x200 choice

WORKOUT #29A total distance - 2,100 yards

WARM-UP = 700 yards, consisting of:
1x200 easy swim
4x50 kick w/fins (use different kicks)
4x50 drills w/fins (use different drills)
1x100 7/3/7 drill

MAIN SET = 1,300 yards, consisting of:
1x300 moderate to strong swim
1x100 easy pull
1x200 moderate to strong swim
1x100 easy pull
1x150 moderate to strong swim
1x100 easy pull
1x100 strong swim
1x100 easy pull
1x50 fast swim
1x100 easy pull

COOL DOWN - 1x100 choice

WORKOUT #29B total distance - 3,100 yards

WARM-UP = 900 yards, consisting of:
1x300 easy swim
6x50 drills w/fins (mix up your drills)
1x300 7/3/7 drill

MAIN SET = 2,000 yards, consisting of:
1x400 strong swim
1x100 easy pull

2x200 descend
1x100 easy pull

4x100 on an interval
1x100 easy pull

8x50 on an interval
1x100 easy pull

COOL DOWN - 1x200 choice

WORKOUT#30A total distance - 2,100 yards

WARM-UP = 800 yards, consisting of:
1x100 easy swim
1x100 easy pull
2x75 w/fins (each 75 consists of 25 left arm / 25 right arm / 25 swim)
3x100 freestyle kick w/fins (1st 100 easy, 2nd 100 fast, 3rd 100 easy)
3x50 freestyle kick w/fins (1st 50 easy, 2nd 50 fast, 3rd 50 easy)

MAIN SET = 1,200 yards, consisting of:
3x50 build
1x150 easy pull

3x50 descend
1x150 easy pull

Repeat above 600

COOL DOWN - 1x100 choice

WORKOUT #30B total distance - 3,100 yards

WARM-UP = 800 yards, consisting of:
1x200 easy swim
2x75 w/fins (each 75 consists of 25 left arm, 25 right arm, 25 swim)
3x100 freestyle kick w/fins (1st 100 easy, 2nd 100 fast, 3rd 100 easy)
3x50 freestyle kick w/fins (1st 50 fast, 2nd 50 easy, 3rd 50 fast)

MAIN SET = 2,200 yards, consisting of:
2x100 build
1x100 easy pull
2x100 descend
1x100 easy pull

3x50 build
1x100 easy pull
3x50 descend
1x100 easy pull

Repeat the above 1,100 yards

COOL DOWN - 1x100 choice

WORKOUT #31A total distance - 2,000 yards

WARM-UP = 800 yards, consisting of:
1x200 easy swim
8x75 w/fins (each 75 - kick 25/ drill 25/ swim 25)

MAIN SET = 1,100 yards, consisting of:
2x100 descend
1x100 easy pull
3x50 descend
1x100 easy pull

2x100 on an interval
1x100 easy pull
3x50 on an interval
1x100 easy pull

COOL DOWN - 1x100 choice

WORKOUT #31B total distance - 3,100 yards

WARM-UP = 900 yards, consisting of:
1x300 easy swim
8x75 w/fins (each 75 - kick 25/ drill 25/ swim 25)

MAIN SET = 2,000 yards, consisting of:
3x200 descend
1x200 easy pull
3x100 descend
1x100 easy pull
3x50 descend
1x50 easy pull

3x100 on an interval
1x100 easy pull
3x50 on an interval
1x50 easy pull

COOL DOWN - 1x200 choice

WORKOUT #32A total distance - 2,200 yards

WARM-UP = 1,100 yards, consisting of:
1x200 easy swim
4x150 w/fins (drill50/swim50/drill50, on each 150. Mix up the drills.)
6x50 kick/swims w/fins

MAIN SET = 1000 yards, consisting of:
2x100 descend
1x100 easy pull

2x100 rest interval
1x100 easy pull

2x50 descend
1x100 easy pull

2x50 on an interval
1x100 easy pull

COOL DOWN - 1x100 choice

WORKOUT#32B total distance - 3,000 yards

WARM-UP = 1,100 yards, consisting of:
1x200 easy swim
12x50 w/fins. (keep alternating, 50 drill / 50 very fast swim)
6x50 kick/swims w/fins

MAIN SET = 1,700 yards, consisting of:
3x100 on an interval
1x100 easy pull

3x100 descend
1x100 easy pull

4x50 on an interval
1x100 easy pull

4x50 descend
1x100 easy pull

4x50 alternating, fast 50 / easy 50
1x100 easy pull

COOL DOWN - 1x200 easy swim

WORKOUT #33A total distance - 2,100 yards

WARM-UP = 700 yards, consisting of:
1x200 easy swim
1x100 easy pull
8x50 drill/swims w/fins

MAIN SET = 1,200 yards, consisting of:
4x50 freestyle KICK w/fins rest interval
1x200 easy pull
3x50 freestyle KICK w/fins rest interval
1x200 easy pull
2x50 freestyle KICK w/fins rest interval
1x200 easy pull

3x50 swim (1st 50 fast, 2nd 50 easy, 3rd 50 fast)

COOL DOWN - 1x200 choice

WORKOUT #33B total distance - 3,050 yards

WARM-UP = 700 yards, consisting of:
1x400 easy swim
6x50 drill/swims w/fins

MAIN SET = 2,150 yards, consisting of:
(Establish a kick interval time the same way you determined your swim interval time)
  6x50 freestyle KICK w/fins on an interval
  1x200 easy pull

  4x50 freestyle KICK w/fins on an interval
  1x200 easy pull

  3x50 freestyle KICK w/fins on an interval
  1x200 easy pull

  2x50 freestyle KICK w/fins on an interval
  1x200 easy pull

  3x100 swim interval
  1x100 easy pull
  2x100 swim descend

COOL DOWN - 1x200 choice

WORKOUT #34A total distance - 2,000 yards

WARM-UP = 1,000 yards, consisting of:
1x200 easy swim
1x200 easy pull
1x100 easy swim
1x100 catch-up drill w/fins
1x100 kick w/fins
1x100 one arm swimming drill w/fins (switch arms every 25)
1x100 kick w/fins
1x100 fingertip drag drill w/fins

MAIN SET = 800 yards
Locomotive set
1x25fast,1x25easy; 1x50fast,1x50easy; 1x75fast,1x75easy;
1x100fast,1x100easy;
1x75fast,1x75easy; 1x50fast,1x50easy; 1x25fast,1x25easy
As much as possible, swim this set, non-stop. Hopefully you will recover from the fast swims during the easy swims. This is referred to as an "active recovery".

COOL DOWN - 1x200 choice

WORKOUT #34B total distance - 3,000 yards

WARM-UP = 800 yards, consisting of:
1x300 swim
1x100 catch-up drill w/fins
1x100 kick w/fins
1x100 fingertip drag drill w/fins
1x100 kick w/fins
1x100 one arm swimming drill w/fins (switch arms every 25)

MAIN SET = 2,000 yards
1,000 yard Locomotive set
1x25fast,1x25easy; 1x50fast,1x50easy; 1x75fast,1x75easy;
1x100fast,1x100easy;
1x100fast,1x100easy; 1x75fast,1x75easy; 1x50fast,1x50easy;
1x25fast,1x25easy
Try to swim this locomotive set, non-stop. Recover from the fast swims on your easy swims. This is referred to as an "active recovery."

PULL above 1,000 yard locomotive set.

COOL DOWN - 1x200 choice

WORKOUT #35A total distance - 2,000 yards

WARM-UP = 800 yards, consisting of:
1x200 easy swim
1x200 7/3/7 drill w/fins
2x100 drill/swims w/fins (each 100, 50 drill/50 swim)
2x100 kick/swims w/fins (each 100, 50 kick/50 swim)

MAIN SET = 1,100 yards, consisting of:
6x50 build
1x50 easy pull

5x50 alternating, fast 50/easy 50
1x50 easy pull

4x50 on an interval
1x50 easy pull

3x50 descend
1x50 easy pull

COOL DOWN - 1x100 choice

WORKOUT #35B total distance - 3,000 yards

WARM-UP = 800 yards, consisting of:
1x300 easy swim
1x100 kick/swims w/fins (50 kick/50 swim)
1x200 7/3/7 drill w/fins
2x100 drill/swims w/fins (50 drill/50 swim, on each 100)

MAIN SET = 2,000 yards, consisting of:
3x300:
1st 300 is 50 fast/250 easy

2nd 300 is 75 fast/225 easy

3rd 300 is 100 fast/200 easy
1x100 easy pull

3x200:
1st 200 is 50 fast/150 easy

2nd 200 is 75 fast/125 easy

3rd 200 is 100 fast/100 easy
1x100 easy pull

3x100:
1st 100 is 25 fast/75 easy

2nd 100 is 50 fast/50 easy

3rd 100 is 75 fast/25 easy

COOL DOWN - 1x200 choice

WORKOUT #36A total distance - 2,000 yards

WARM-UP = 900 yards, consisting of:
1x300 easy swim
6x50 kick w/fins rest interval
3x100 drills w/fins (3 different drills, 100 of each)

MAIN SET = 900 yards, consisting of:
2x100 descend
1x50 easy swim

2x75 descend
1x50 easy swim

2x50 descend
1x50 easy swim

2x25 descend
1x50 easy swim

2x100 hypoxic pull (try 5,2,4,3 breathing pattern on each 100)

COOL DOWN - 1x200 choice

WORKOUT #36B total distance - 3,000 yards

WARM-UP = 900 yards, consisting of:
1x300 easy swim
6x50 kick w/fins interval
3x100 drills w/fins (3 different drills, 100 of each)

MAIN SET = 1,850 yards, consisting of:
4x150 on an interval
1x50 easy swim or pull

4x100 on an interval
1x50 easy swim or pull

4x75 on an interval
1x50 easy swim or pull

4x50 on an interval
1x50 easy swim or pull

4x25 on an interval
1x50 easy swim or pull

COOL DOWN - 1x250 choice

WORKOUT #37A total distance - 2000 yards

WARM-UP = 1,100 yards, consisting of:
1x200 easy swim
1x200 easy pull
5x100 w/fins (1st,3rd &5th 100, drill. 2nd &4th 100, swim Fast)
4x50 kick/drills w/fins

MAIN SET = 800 yards, consisting of:
4x100:
1st 100, easy
2nd 100, build
3rd 100, easy pull
4th 100, fast

4x50:
1st 50, easy
2nd 50, build
3rd 50, easy pull
4th 50, fast
Repeat above 4x50 set

COOL DOWN - 1x100 easy pull

WORKOUT #37B total distance - 3,100 yards

WARM-UP = 900 yards, consisting of:
1x400 easy swim
5x100 w/fins (1st, 3rd & 5th 100, drill / 2nd & 4th 100, swim fast.)

MAIN SET = 2,000 yards, consisting of:
4x200:
1st 200 easy
2nd 200 build (within the 200, swim a little faster on each of the four 50s)
3rd 200 easy pull
4th 200 fast

4x150:
1st 150 easy
2nd 150 build (within the 150, swim a little faster on each of the three 50s)
3rd 150 easy pull
4th 150 fast

4x100:
1st 100 easy
2nd 100 build (within the 100, swim a little faster on each of the four 25s)
3rd 100 easy pull
4th 100 fast

4x50:
1st 50 easy
2nd 50 build (swim the second 25 a little faster then the first)
3rd 50 easy pull
4th 50 fast

COOL DOWN = 1x200 easy pull

WORKOUT #38A total distance - 2,000 yards

WARM-UP = 700 yards, consisting of:
1x200 easy swim
4x100 kick w/fins (each 100, 50 fast/50 easy)
1x100 easy pull

MAIN SET = 1,150 yards, consisting of:
3x100 on an interval
1x100 easy pull
3x50 on an interval
1x100 easy pull

2x100 on an interval
1x100 easy pull
2x50 on an interval
1x100 easy pull

COOL DOWN - 1x150 choice

WORKOUT #38B total distance - 3,100 yards

WARM-UP = 500 yards, consisting of:
1x300 easy swim
2x100 kick w/fins (each 100, 50 fast/50 easy)

MAIN SET = 2,400 yards, consisting of:
5x100 on an interval
1x100 easy swim or pull
5x50 on an interval
1x100 easy swim or pull

4x100 on an interval
1x100 easy swim or pull
4x50 on an interval
1x100 easy swim or pull

3x100 on an interval
1x100 easy swim or pull
3x50 on an interval
1x100 easy swim or pull

COOL DOWN - 1x200 choice

WORKOUT #39A total distance - 2,000 yards

WARM-UP = 600 yards, consisting of:
1x200 easy swim (count your strokes for each 25 yds.)
1x200 easy pull
1x200 easy swim (Long strokes. Try to reduce above stroke count)

MAIN SET = 1,200 yards, consisting of:
1x200 easy to moderate swim
1x100 easy pull
1x200 descend the above 1x200 easy to moderate swim
1x100 easy pull

1x100 easy to moderate swim
1x100 easy pull
1x100 descend the above 1x100 easy to moderate swim
1x100 easy pull

4x50 (alternate fast25/easy25, on each 50)

COOL DOWN - 1x200 easy swim

WORKOUT #39B total distance - 3,000 yards

WARM-UP = 600 yards, consisting of:
1x200 easy swim (count your strokes for each 25 yds.)
1x200 easy pull
1x200 easy swim (Long strokes. Try to reduce above stroke count)

MAIN SET = 2,100 yards, consisting of:
1x300 strong
1x100 easy pull
1x300 descend the above 1x300 strong swim
1x100 easy pull

1x200 strong
1x100 easy pull
1x200 descend the above 1x200 strong swim
1x100 easy pull

1x100 strong
1x100 easy pull
1x100 descend the above 1x100 strong swim
1x100 easy pull

6x50 alternating, 50 fast/50 easy

COOL DOWN - 1x300 choice

WORKOUT #40A total distance - 2,200 yards

WARM-UP = 800 yards, consisting of:
1x200 easy swim
1x200 w/fins (50 kick, 50 drill, 50 swim, 50 drill)
Repeat above 200 w/fins, **2** more times

MAIN SET = 1,200 yards, consisting of:
1x50 fast
1x50 easy pull
2x50 on an interval
1x100 easy pull
3x50 on an interval
1x150 easy pull

2x100 on an interval
1x200 easy pull
1x100 fast
1x100 easy pull

COOL DOWN - 1x200 choice

WORKOUT #40B total distance - 3,200 yards

WARM-UP = 800 yards, consisting of:
1x200 easy swim
1x200 w/fins (50 kick, 50 drill, 50 swim, 50 drill)
Repeat above 200 set w/fins, **2** more times

MAIN SET = 2,200 yards, consisting of:
1x50 fast
1x50 easy pull
2x50 on an interval
1x100 easy pull
3x50 on an interval
1x150 easy pull
4x50 on an interval
1x200 easy pull

3x100 on an interval
1x300 easy pull
2x100 on an interval
1x200 easy pull
1x100 fast
1x100 easy pull

COOL DOWN - 1x200 choice

WORKOUT #41A total distance = 2,100 yards

WARM-UP = 400 yards, consisting of:
1x200 easy swim
1x100 kick w/fins
1x100 drill w/fins

MAIN SET = 1,600 yards, consisting of:
800 yard locomotive set
1x25 fast
1x25 easy
1x50 fast
1x50 easy
1x75 fast
1x75 easy
1x100 fast
1x100 easy
1x75 fast
1x75 easy
1x50 fast
1x50 easy
1x25 fast
1x25 easy
Repeat above locomotive set, **PULLING**.
Try your best to do each locomotive set, non-stop.

COOL DOWN - 1x100 easy swim

WORKOUT #41B total distance - 3,100 yards

WARM-UP = 500 yards, consisting of:
1x200 easy swim
1x150 kick w/fins
1x150 drill w/fins

MAIN SET = 2,400 yards, consisting of:
Three 800 yard locomotive sets
Check #41A above, for instructions on an 800 locomotive set

KICK one locomotive set w/fins, non-stop

PULL one locomotive set, non-stop

SWIM one locomotive set, non-stop

COOL DOWN - 1x200 choice

WORKOUT #42A total distance - 2,000 yards

WARM-UP = 800 yards, consisting of:
1x200 easy swim
6x100 w/fins (each 100 is 25kick/75 drill)

MAIN SET = 1,100 yards, consisting of:
2x50 on the tightest or toughest interval you can make.
1x100 easy pull

3x50 add 5 seconds to the above interval. If for example the 2x50 interval was 1:30, make this interval time,1:35.
1x100 easy pull

4x50 interval (add 10 seconds to the 2x50 interval time)
1x100 easy pull

5x50 interval (add 15 seconds to the 2x50)
1x100 easy pull

COOL DOWN - 1x100 choice

WORKOUT #42B total distance - 3,000 yards

WARM-UP = 600 yards, consisting of:
1x200 easy swim
4x100 w/fins (each 100 is 25 kick/75 drill)

MAIN SET = 2,200 yards, consisting of:
4x100 on the tightest interval time you can make
1x200 easy pull

6x100 add 5 seconds to the 4x100 interval time
1x200 easy pull

8x100 add 10 seconds to the 4x100 interval time

COOL DOWN - 1x200 easy pull

WORKOUT#43A total distance - 2,050 yards

WARM-UP = 600 yards, consisting of:
1x200 easy swim
3x100 KLRS w/fins
1x100 easy pull

MAIN SET = 1,250 yards, consisting of:
1x100 freestyle kick easy to moderate speed. (fins optional)
1x200 moderate swim
1x200 easy pull

1x100 freestyle kick easy to moderate speed. (fins optional)
1x100 strong swim
1x200 easy pull

1x100 freestyle kick easy to moderate speed. (fins optional)
1x50 fast swim
1x200 easy pull

COOL DOWN - 1x200 choice

WORKOUT #43B total distance - 3,000 yards

WARM-UP = 700 yards, consisting of:
1x400 easy swim
3x100 KLRS w/fins

MAIN SET = 2,200 yards, consisting of:
1x100 easy to moderate freestyle kick (fins optional)
1x500 strong swim
1x100 easy pull

1x100 easy to moderate freestyle kick (fins optional)
1x400 strong swim
1x100 easy pull

1x100 easy to moderate freestyle kick (fins optional)
1x300 strong swim
1x100 easy pull

1x100 easy to moderate freestyle kick (fins optional)
1x200 fast swim
1x100 easy pull

COOL DOWN - 1x100 choice

WORKOUT #44A total distance - 2,100 yards

WARM-UP = 800 yards, consisting of:
1x200 easy swim
1x200 kick with fins (mix up some different kicks)
1x200 drill with fins (mix up some different drills)
1x200 fast swim with fins (get moving here. It is good to get the feeling of speed)

MAIN SET = 1,200 yards, consisting of:
2x100 descend (second 100 a few seconds faster then the first 100)
1x200 easy pull

6x50 rest interval
1x300 easy pull

3x50 descend
1x50 easy pull

COOL DOWN - 1x100 easy swim

WORKOUT#44B total distance - 3,100 yards

WARM-UP = 800 yards. Same as above (#44A)

MAIN SET = 2,100 yards, consisting of:
3x200 descend
1x100 easy pull

6x100 on an interval
1x100 easy pull

3x50 descend
1x50 easy pull

3x50 descend
1x50 easy pull

4x50 on an interval
1x100 pull

COOL DOWN - 1x200 easy swim

WORKOUT #45A total distance - 2,000 yards

WARM-UP = 700 yards, consisting of:
1x200 easy swim
2x200 w/fins (each 200, 50kick/50 left arm/ 50right arm/50catch-up)
1x100 easy pull

MAIN SET = 1,200 yards, consisting of:
1x25 fast swim
1x50 easy swim
1x75 fast swim
1x100 easy swim
1x75 fast swim
1x50 easy swim
1x25 fast swim

Repeat the above 400 set **Pulling**
Repeat the above 400 set **Swimming**, again

COOL DOWN - 1x100 choice

WORKOUT #45B total distance - 3,000 yards

WARM-UP = 500 yards, consisting of:
1x300 easy swim
1x200 w/fins (50kick/50left arm/50right arm/50catch-up)

MAIN SET = 2,400 yards, consisting of:
1x25 fast swim
1x50 easy swim
1x75 fast swim
1x100 easy swim
1x150 fast swim
1x200 easy swim

1x200 fast swim
1x150 easy swim
1x100 fast swim
1x75 easy swim
1x50 fast swim
1x25 easy swim

Repeat the above 1,200 set, **Pulling**

COOL DOWN - 1x100 choice

WORKOUT #46A total distance - 2,100 yards

WARM-UP = 600 yards, consisting of:
1x200 easy swim
2x100 w/fins (ea.100 consists of 25 left arm/ 25 right arm/ 50 swim)
2x100 w/fins (ea.100 consists of 25 catch-up/25 fingertip drag/ 50 swim)

MAIN SET = 1,300 yards
(During this main set we are going to be ASCENDING interval Sets. Example: 2x100 leaving on 2:20 and then ascend the next 2x100 interval set, by leaving on 2:25. Therefore, the intervals are becoming easier.)

2x100 swim the tightest interval you can.
1x100 easy pull

2x100 Ascend above interval by 5 seconds
1x100 easy pull

4x50 interval
1x50 easy pull

4x50 Ascend above interval by 5 seconds
1x50 easy pull

4x50 interval Ascend above interval by 5 seconds

COOL DOWN - 1x200 easy pull

WORKOUT #46B total distance - 3,100 yards

WARM-UP = 700 yards, consisting of:
1x200 easy swim
2x100 w/fins (ea. 100 consists of 25 left arm/ 25 right arm/50 swim)
2x50 kick/swims w/fins
2x100 w/fins (ea. 100 consists of 25 catch-up/ 25 fingertip drag/ 50 swim)

MAIN SET = 2,200 yards
(In this main set, we are going to be ASCENDING interval sets. Example: 4x100 leaving on 2:00 and then ascend the next interval set by leaving on 2:05 and the next on 2:10. Therefore, the intervals are getting easier.)

4x100 interval (the fastest interval you can hold)
1x100 easy pull

4x100 interval (Ascend above interval by 5 seconds)
1x100 easy pull

4x100 interval (Ascend above interval by 5 seconds)
1x100 easy pull

4x50 interval (fastest interval you can hold)
1x50 easy pull

4x50 interval (Ascend above interval by 5 seconds)
1x50 easy pull

4x50 interval (Ascend above interval by 5 seconds)

COOL DOWN - 1x200 choice

WORKOUT #47A total distance - 2,175 yards

WARM-UP = 1,000 yards, consisting of:
1x200 easy swim
6x50 kick/swims w/fins
6x50 drill/swims w/fins
1x200 7/3/7 drill w/fins

MAIN SET = 975 yards, consisting of:
3x100 (1st 100, easy/ 2nd 100, fast/ 3rd 100, easy pull)

3x75 (1st 75, easy/ 2nd 75, fast/ 3rd 75, easy pull)

3x50 (1st 50, easy/ 2nd 50, fast/ 3rd 50, easy pull)
REPEAT the 3x50 set, **2** more times

COOL DOWN - 1x200 choice

WORKOUT #47B total distance - 3,050 yards

WARM-UP = 900 yards, consisting of:
1x300 easy swim
4x50 kick/swims w/fins (kick fast 25/swim easy 25 on these kick/swims)
4x50 drill/swims w/fins
1x200 7/3/7 drill w/fins

MAIN SET = 1,950 yards, consisting of:
3x300 (1st 300, easy/ 2nd 300, fast/ 3rd 300, easy pull)

3x200 (1st 200, easy/ 2nd 200, fast,/ 3rd 200, easy pull)

3x100 (1st 100, easy/ 2nd 100, fast/ 3rd 100, easy pull)

3x50 (1st 50, easy/ 2nd 50, fast,/ 3rd 50, easy pull)

COOL DOWN = 1x200 choice

WORKOUT #48A total distance - 2,000 yards

WARM-UP = 1,000 yards, consisting of:
1x300 easy swim
1x200 kick w/fins (100 moderate, 100 easy)
1x200 drill w/fins (2 drills, 100 of each)
1x300 easy pull

MAIN SET = 700 yards, consisting of:
14x50:

1st, 2nd & 3rd 50, descend
4th 50, easy

5th & 6th 50, on an interval
7th 50, easy

8th, 9th & 10th 50, descend
11th 50, easy

12th & 13th 50, descend
14th 50, easy

COOL DOWN = 300 yards, consisting of:
1x200 easy pull
1x100 easy swim

WORKOUT #48B total distance - 3,050 yards

WARM-UP = 1,000 yards, consisting of:
1x300 easy swim
1x200 kick w/fins (100 fast, 100 easy)
1x200 drill w/fins
1x300 easy pull

MAIN SET = 1,850 yards, consisting of:
11x100:
1st through 3rd 100, descend
4th 100, easy

5th & 6th 100, descend
7th 100, easy

8th through 10th 100, descend
11th 100, easy

11x50:
1st through 3rd 50, descend
4th 50, easy

5th & 6th 50, descend
7th 50, easy

8th through 10th 50, descend
11th 50, easy

1x200 hypoxic pull (you pick the breathing pattern - 50 yards of each)

COOL DOWN - 1x200 easy swim

WORKOUT #49A total distance - 2,000 yards

WARM-UP = 1,000 yards, consisting of:
1x200 easy swim
1x100 easy pull
1x100 kick w/ fins
4x50 drill w/fins (4different drills, 50 yds. of each)
Repeat the above 4x50-drill set, **2** more times

MAIN SET = 900 yards, consisting of:
2x50 on an interval
1x50 easy pull

2x100 rest interval
1x100 easy pull

2x100 rest interval
1x100 easy pull

2x50 on an interval
1x50 easy pull

COOL DOWN - 1x100 choice

WORKOUT #49B total distance - 3,050 yards

WARM-UP = 550 yards, consisting of:
1x150 easy swim
1x100 kick w/fins (flutter kick)
2x50 drill w/fins (2 different drills)
Repeat above 1x100 kick & 2x50 drill

MAIN SET = 2,400 yards, consisting of:
3x50 on an interval
1x50 easy pull

4x75 on an interval
1x100 easy pull

5x100 on an interval
1x100 easy pull

Repeat 5x100 interval &1x100 easy pull

4x75 on an interval
1x100 easy pull

3x50 on an interval
1x50 easy pull

COOL DOWN - 1x100 choice

WORKOUT #50A total distance - 2,100 yards

WARM-UP = 700 yards, consisting of:
1x100 easy swim
1x200 w/fins (kick 50, 1 arm drill 50, catch-up 50, swim 50)
Repeat above 200 w/fins, **2** more times

MAIN SET = 1,300 yards, consisting of:
1x100 easy swim

3x75 descend
1x25 easy swim

3x50 descend
1x100 easy pull

1x100 easy swim

2x75 descend
1x50 easy pull

2x50 descend
1x100 easy pull

1x100 easy swim

1x75 fast
1x25 easy

COOL DOWN - 1x100 choice

WORKOUT #50B total distance - 3,000 yards

WARM-UP = 700 yards, consisting of:
1x300 easy swim
1x200 w/fins (kick 50, 1 arm drill 50, catch-up 50, kick & balance drill 50)
Repeat above 200 w/fins set

MAIN SET = 2,100 yards, consisting of:
1x200 easy to moderate swim

3x150 descend
1x50 easy pull

3x100 descend
1x50 easy pull

3x50 descend
1x50 easy pull

1x100 easy to moderate swim

2x150 descend
1x50 easy pull

2x100 descend
1x50 easy pull

2x50 descend
1x50 easy pull

COOL DOWN - 1x200 choice

30 MINUTE CHALLENGE WORKOUT

Check the total distance you can swim in 30 minutes. It would be best if you can have a friend watch the time and count your lengths, to determine your distance. It is very difficult to keep an accurate count by yourself. Keep a record of your distance.

A good way to monitor your progress is to do this 30-minute swim, every 3 months.

HAVE FUN!
and remember
You don't stop swimming because you get old.
You get old because you stop swimming.

Swimming_for_life@yahoo.com
http://www.geocities.com/swimming_for_life

Printed in the United States
117499LV00005B/187/A